THE CANDLE
CLASSIC BIBLE

presented to

....

from

....

date

....

THE CANDLE
CLASSIC
BIBLE

CANDLE
BOOKS

The Candle Classic Bible
Illustrations copyright © Bill Noller International Publishing, San Dimas, CA. 91773
This edition copyright © 2012 Lion Hudson plc

Published in 2012 by Candle Books, a publishing imprint of Lion Hudson plc.

Distributed in the UK by Marston Book Services Ltd,
PO Box 269, Abingdon, Oxon OX14 4YN
Distributed in the USA by Kregel Publications,
PO Box 2607, Grand Rapids, Michigan 49501

Worldwide co-edition organized and produced by Lion Hudson plc,
Wilkinson House, Jordan Hill Road, Oxford OX2 8DR, England.
Tel: +44 (0) 1865 302750 Fax: +44 (0) 1865 302757
Email: coed@lionhudson.com www.lionhudson.com

ISBN 978 1 85985 867 7

First printing March 2012, China

CONTENTS
THE OLD TESTAMENT

The Story of the Israelites

The Story of the Judges

THE NEW TESTAMENT

THE OLD TESTAMENT

1

The World is God's Creation

Genesis 1–2

A long time ago, God made the world. It was dark and empty, and nothing lived in it. Then came six days of Creation. This is what happened.

On the first day God said, "Let there be light," and light came. God called the light day. At the end of the day, darkness returned, and God called it night.

On the second day God placed the sky above the earth and called it heaven.

On the third day God divided the water-covered earth into rivers, lakes, and oceans. He made dry land appear between them. Then he made plants grow on the land. On the fourth day God made the big bright sun to shine during the day. He made the moon and sparkling stars to shine at night.

On the fifth day God made fish and other sea creatures. Then he made waterbirds, like ducks and geese, and other birds, like robins and eagles, that live high in the trees. On the sixth day God made animals.

He made huge ones, like elephants, and tiny ones, like mice. Some were beautiful, like the tiger. Others were funny looking, like the anteater. Some, like the cheetah, could run fast. Others, like the turtle, walked very slowly. And God made insects – some that flew, some that crawled, and some that jumped.

2

God Makes the First People

Genesis 1–2

While it was still the sixth day, God decided to make a man. God took dust from the ground and formed it into a man's body. He breathed into it, and the man became alive. God named him Adam. Adam was different from the animals because he was like God himself.

God gave Adam a home in a beautiful garden called Eden. It was full of wonderful fruit trees. God said, "Adam, you may eat any fruit except the fruit from this one tree, the Tree of the Knowledge of Good and Evil. If you even taste this tree's fruit, you will die."

God put Adam in charge of the Garden. He told Adam to give each kind of animal, bird, and insect a name.

God knew it wasn't good for Adam to be the only person in the world. He needed a companion. So God made a woman from one of Adam's ribs.

So the earth and skies, plants and animals, and human beings were finished in six days. God was very pleased with everything he had made.

On the seventh day God didn't make anything. It was a quiet, holy day of rest.

3

The Saddest Day on Earth

Genesis 3

Satan was in the Garden of Eden as well as God and Adam and his wife. Satan is an evil spirit who tries to get people to do wrong things. Satan disguised himself as a snake, or serpent. He asked the woman, "Did God tell you not to eat any fruit in the Garden?"

"No!" she replied. "We can eat from every tree except the Tree of the Knowledge of Good and Evil. If we eat that fruit, we will die."

"No, you won't!" Satan told her. "It can't hurt you. It will make you wise like God!"

Then the woman made a big mistake. She looked at the tree. The fruit looked so good! She remembered

that Satan had said it would make her wise, so she disobeyed God and ate some of the fruit. Then she gave some to Adam to eat.

Later they heard God calling them. They didn't answer. Instead, they hid among the trees because they were afraid of him. God called again. "Where are you, Adam?"

"I'm hiding," Adam finally replied. "I'm afraid of you."

"Why? Did you eat the fruit I told you not to eat?" God asked.

Adam blamed his wife. "The woman brought me some, and I ate it."

God asked the woman, "Did you really do that?"

"I did, because the serpent tricked me," she said.

What weak excuses for disobeying God.

4

Disobedience Brings Punishment

Genesis 3

Because Adam and his wife listened to the serpent instead of to God, God punished them. First, God told the serpent, "From now on, you will have to crawl on the dusty ground. You will be a special enemy of the woman and her children. You will strike at their heels, but they will crush your head."

Then God told the woman that because she had disobeyed, she would suffer pain when her children were born.

God said to Adam, "Because you ate the fruit I told you not to eat, you will have to work hard to grow crops. Then you will die, and your body will return to the ground from which I made it."

After that Adam named his wife Eve. Her name meant she would become the first mother of all the people who would later live on the earth.

God made Adam and Eve leave the beautiful Garden of Eden for fear that they might also eat from the Tree of Life and live forever in their sinfulness. Then he sent angels with swords to guard the entrance to the Garden and to the Tree of Life.

5

The World's First Murder

Genesis 4

Eve gave birth to two sons, Cain and Abel. Cain became a farmer, and Abel became a shepherd. When it was time to offer God a gift, Cain brought grain and fruit, and Abel sacrificed a lamb. God was pleased with Abel's offering, but he

saw that Cain had disobedience in his heart, so he didn't accept Cain's gifts. Cain became very angry.

"Why are you so angry?" God asked him. "If you do what is right, I will be pleased with you, too. If you don't, you will always be in trouble because of your sin."

Cain became more angry with God, and he hated Abel because God had accepted Abel's sacrifice and not his. One day the brothers went out to the field together where Cain attacked Abel and killed him.

God called to Cain: "Where is your brother?"

"How should I know?" Cain answered crossly. "Am I supposed to look after him all the time?"

God knows everything we do, and he knew that Cain had killed Abel. He said, "Your brother's blood calls out to me from the ground. Now you must leave home and wander from place to place. You will live in fear, and your crops will never grow well."

6
The Man Who Walked with God

Genesis 5

Adam lived until he was 930 years old. He and Eve had many children and grandchildren and great-grandchildren. Soon many, many people lived in the world.

One of them was Enoch. The Bible tells us Enoch loved God and thought about him all the time. Enoch and God were friends, and Enoch pleased God by obeying him in every way.

When Enoch was 365 years old, God took him to live with him. We don't know how it happened, but we know Enoch didn't have to die like other people.

Enoch had a son named Methuselah, who lived to be 969 years old. As far as we know, he was the oldest man who has ever lived.

7
A Good Man in a Sinful World

Genesis 6

As time went on, people became more and more sinful. They didn't care about pleasing God or obeying him. God kept warning them, but they didn't pay any attention. This made God very angry. He said, "I am going to destroy

them by sending a great flood of water to cover the earth. Everyone will drown, all the people, animals, snakes, birds, and insects – everything."

But there was one man, Noah, who loved God and served him. God wanted to save Noah and his family from the flood. He told Noah to build a very large boat, as high as a three-storey house, with a long window reaching all around it, just under the roof.

The boat would be big enough for Noah, his wife, their three sons, Shem, Ham, and Japheth, and their wives. It would also have room for many animals – at least two of every kind, as well as birds, reptiles, and insects.

ark, and made it as long, as wide, and as high as God had said. It took him about a hundred years.

When the ark was finished, God told Noah to gather the animals and food for many weeks. Noah was to take a male and a female of some kinds of animals so babies would be born. Of other kinds he was to take seven pairs – some for eating and some for sacrificing when they could leave the ark.

Noah obeyed God's instructions. He took his family and the animals into the ark. About a week later, the flood began. Rain poured down, and the floodwaters rose up until there was enough water

---

8

Noah Obeys Orders

Genesis 7

Noah did exactly what God told him. He built the boat, sometimes called an

to make the huge ark float. Every creature left outside the ark drowned – men, women, and children, animals, birds, reptiles, and insects.

But because Noah and his family had obeyed God's warning, they were safe inside the ark, floating on top of the water.

9
A Long Boat Ride
Genesis 8

Rain kept falling for more than a month, but Noah and his family stayed dry inside their boat. They must have been glad that they had listened to God and obeyed him! Finally the rain stopped, and very slowly the water began to go down again. Noah and his family stayed inside the ark for 150 days. By that time the water had gone down enough for the boat to touch the ground, up in some mountains called Ararat. Still they stayed inside, waiting for God to tell them when it was safe to get out.

Noah sent a raven out of the boat. It kept flying around until the ground became dry. Then he sent out a dove. The dove came back, so Noah waited for about a week and then sent it out again. This time it returned carrying an olive leaf in its bill, showing that the water had gone down to the level of the trees. After another week he sent the dove out once more, and this time it didn't come back. In a few more weeks the ground became dry enough to walk on. Then God said, "Noah, it is time to leave the boat."

10
Dry Land at Last
Genesis 8–9

Noah let all the animals, birds, snakes, and insects out of their stalls and cages onto the dry ground. Then Noah and his family left the ark too. First of all Noah and his sons built an altar and worshipped God. They thanked him for saving them from the flood. They sacrificed some of the extra animals they had taken onto the boat. God was happy that they wanted to worship him, and he was pleased with their sacrifice. God said to himself, "Although people will disobey me again, I will never send another flood."

God told Noah and his sons to have many children so the earth would again be full of people. He said they would be able to use animals and other creatures for food and for doing work.

Then God told Noah about his decision not to use a flood again to wipe out the people and animals on earth. He said, "When it rains, don't be afraid of another flood, but look up at the sky. There you will see a beautiful rainbow. It will remind you of my promise to you and to your children after you."

11
The Tower of Babel

Genesis 11

After the flood ended, Noah's sons had many children and grandchildren. Sadly, they did things that displeased God just like the people who had lived before the flood. Nowadays people speak many different languages, but in Noah's day everyone spoke the same

language. They wanted to live together and decided to build a huge tower that would reach up into the sky. They said, "This tower will show how great we are. We can stay together and not get spread out across the earth."

This was against God's command to occupy the earth and take care of it. God was displeased when he saw the tower they were building. He decided to stop them by making them speak in different languages so they couldn't understand one another! This made them angry, and they gave up trying to work together, leaving the tower unfinished. The tower is called the Tower of Babel. Babel means "mixed-

up" or "confused". The languages were mixed up and so were the people! Finally, small groups who could speak to each other moved away from the ones who spoke other languages, and so the people scattered to all parts of the earth.

12
Abram Believes God

Genesis 12

Long ago a man named Abram lived in a large city. Abram and his family believed in God, but their neighbours worshipped idols. One day God told Abram to leave his home and go to a special country that would belong to him and his children. That country was Canaan, and because God promised it to Abram, we call it the Promised Land. Abram believed God, so he took his wife, Sarai, and his nephew, Lot, and they started for Canaan. Abram also had many servants and animals. Having

many animals was like having lots of money – so Abram was very rich.

When they got to Canaan, God said to Abram, "I'm going to give this land to you and to your children forever." Abram thanked God by building an altar and sacrificing an animal on it.

But there was a famine in Canaan. A famine is when crops don't grow because there isn't enough rain, and many people starve to death. Abram took Sarai, Lot, and his servants into Egypt, where there was enough food. When the famine was over, they returned to the Promised Land to live.

13
A Selfish Choice

Genesis 13

Abram had very large herds and flocks of cows, sheep, and goats. Lot had many

animals too. They had servants who took care of their animals, but the two groups of servants quarrelled about the best fields and the best water supply for the animals.

When Abram heard this, he said to Lot, "This is a large country. I will divide the land with you. Then our shepherds won't have to fight over the pasture and the water. Lot, you may have the first choice."

Abram could have kept the best land for himself because God had given it all to him. But he was generous. His nephew, Lot, was not as kind. He chose the best part, close to the River Jordan, where the fields were well watered. But when he chose that part, he also chose to live in the wicked city of Sodom. Later on Lot's selfish choice caused much trouble.

another altar to the Lord. Each time he moved, he built a new altar so he always had a place near him where he could worship God by making sacrifices.

14

A Wonderful Promise

Genesis 13

After Lot had moved away, God made some more wonderful promises to Abram. "Look around you. I am going to give you and your children all the land you can see. Someday even the land Lot chose will be yours too.

And I will give you many children, grandchildren, and great-grandchildren. You will have as many descendants as there are bits of dust on the earth. They will become a great nation, and I will bless them."

That promise has come true. Today we call that great group of people the Jews or Israelis, and the Promised Land, Israel.

Abram moved to Hebron and built

15

Lot is Captured

Genesis 14

About that time, four neighbouring kings made war against Sodom. They won and stole all the money, food, clothing, and jewellery in Sodom. They took some people to become their slaves. Lot was one of them. When Abram heard that Lot was in trouble, he gathered his servants and friends and chased after the army. They caught up with the four kings and started to fight. God let Abram win. He rescued Lot and the other captives.

As they returned to Sodom, Abram was met by Melchizedek, a powerful king who loved God. Melchizedek blessed Abram and prayed for him. Abram gave Melchizedek one-tenth of everything he had taken from the enemy.

The king of Sodom was happy when Abram returned with the captives. He said to Abram, "Give me back my people. You can keep everything else for yourself."

Abram refused. He had promised God he wouldn't keep anything for himself. He wanted everyone to know it was God alone who had made him rich.

16
Sarai Gets Impatient

Genesis 15–16

Abram and Sarai were getting very old. They thought about God's promise to make their children become a great nation, but they were still childless! Abram talked to God about it. God promised Abram a son. God said, "I am your friend, and I will always protect you. Look at all the stars. Can you count them?"

Abram couldn't count all the stars in the sky. No one can. But God said, "Not only will you have a son, but you will have so many grandchildren and great-grandchildren that their families will be like the stars – too many to count!"

Abram believed God, and because he believed, God was very pleased with him.

Sarai became impatient

for the son God had promised. She said her servant girl, Hagar, could be Abram's second wife so a baby could be born into the family. Hagar had a baby boy, Ishmael. But this wasn't the way God had planned for Abram and Sarai to get the promised son – and their disobedience brought much trouble into the family.

17
Abram Gets a New Name

Genesis 17

Several more years went by. God spoke to Abram again and reminded him of the promises he had made to him. God told him they would all come true. He said, "You are to be called Abraham because that means 'father of nations'." God gave Sarai a new name too – Sarah, which means "princess".

Then God made a covenant with Abraham. A covenant is a very important agreement that God makes with people. Part of the covenant was that God would allow Sarah to have a

baby, the promised one to start Abraham's great nation.

Because Abraham thought he and Sarah were too old to have a baby, he said, "You must mean that you are going to bless Ishmael!"

"I will bless him," God replied, "but I mean that Sarah herself will have a baby. You must name him Isaac, which means 'laughter'."

18
Heavenly Visitors

Genesis 18

Abraham was sitting at the door of his tent when he saw three men coming. He gave them water and asked Sarah to prepare food for them. Two of the men were angels, and the third one was God, in the form of a man.

The one who was God said, "Next year you and Sarah will have the promised son." Sarah heard this and laughed at the idea of having a baby in her old age.

God asked Abraham, "Why did Sarah laugh? Doesn't she know that the Lord can do anything?"

Sarah was afraid, so she lied. She said, "I didn't laugh." But God knows everything. He knew she had laughed.

When the three visitors left, Abraham walked with them toward Sodom, where Lot lived. God told Abraham he was planning

to destroy Sodom to punish the people for their wickedness. Abraham didn't want Lot to be destroyed, so he asked God, "If there are fifty good men there, will you change your mind?"

God answered, "Yes."

Abraham kept asking, reducing the number until he got to ten. God agreed to leave the city alone if he could find even ten good men there.

Then Abraham went home.

19
The Angels Warn Lot
Genesis 19

That evening two angels came to warn Lot about the trouble that was coming. They said, "You, your wife and daughters, and their husbands must get out of Sodom quickly because God is going to destroy the city."

Lot's sons-in-law didn't believe the warning and refused to leave. Lot, his wife, and his daughters started to leave. The angels hurried them along. "Don't look back at Sodom," they said. "Run to the mountains and hide."

Lot was afraid to go up into the mountains, so he begged the angels to let him stay in a small nearby city called Zoar. They

said, "All right, but hurry up!"

Lot's wife knew she shouldn't look back at Sodom, but she turned around for a last look. Suddenly she turned into a big pillar of salt!

Lot and his daughters had no time to stop. They hurried on and left her there.

20
God Destroys Sodom
Genesis 19

As Lot and his daughters arrived at Zoar, the sun rose and God poured down fire on Sodom and a nearby city named Gomorrah. Everything burned up, the buildings, people, animals, and plants.

Far away, Abraham could see great billows of smoke rising from those terrible fires. Then he knew God had not been able to find even ten good people in Sodom because God had promised to spare the city if he found ten people who were not wicked.

The people in Zoar weren't much better than the ones in Sodom, and Lot became afraid of them. He decided he would be safer in the mountains, so he and his daughters lived in a cave. His daughters were not good women. They became the mothers of men who started very wicked tribes that made a lot of trouble for God's people many years later.

the boy and his mother go, and I will take care of them. Ishmael, too, shall become a great nation."

So Abraham gave Hagar and Ishmael food and water and sent them into the desert.

22
God Takes Care of Ishmael

Genesis 21

As Hagar and Ishmael walked through the desert, they quickly used up the water Abraham had given them. Hagar didn't know where to find any more water. She was afraid that Ishmael would die of thirst.

21
The Son of Promise

Genesis 21

The following year Sarah had a baby boy. At last Abraham had the son who would start the great nation God had promised him. Abraham and Sarah remembered God's instructions and named the baby Isaac.

Isaac grew, and Abraham gave a party for him. Ishmael, Abraham's older son, who had been born to Hagar, the servant woman, was at the party. He teased his half-brother, Isaac, and this made Sarah angry. She told Abraham he should send Hagar and Ishmael away. Even though it had been Sarah's idea that Abraham have a baby with Hagar, the servant-wife, Sarah had always been jealous of Hagar and Ishmael.

Ishmael was not the son of God's promise, but he was Abraham's little boy, and Abraham didn't like to send him away. God said to Abraham, "Let

She found a bush. Ishmael lay down in its shade. Then Hagar walked away and sat by herself, crying. Ishmael was crying, too, because he was so thirsty. Then the Angel of the Lord said to Hagar, "God has heard your son crying. Don't be afraid. Go back and comfort him." As she was returning to Ishmael, suddenly she saw a well! She filled up the water bottle and gave Ishmael a drink. He felt better, and they were able to continue their trip.

They made their new home in Paran. Ishmael grew up and became an expert with a bow and arrow. He married a girl from Egypt, and they had many descendants who became a great nation, as God had said they would. Just as Ishmael didn't get along well with Isaac, so Ishmael's descendants, the Arabs, have never got along well with Isaac's descendants, the Jews.

23
Abraham Proves His Faith

Genesis 22

One day God told Abraham to take Isaac up to Mount Moriah and offer him as a burnt sacrifice on an altar. Although Abraham loved his son very much, he obeyed. He took Isaac and two servants and started up the mountain, carrying a knife, some wood, and some fire to light the wood. When they could see the place of sacrifice ahead, Abraham left the servants, and he and Isaac went on. Isaac asked Abraham, "Father, where is the lamb we are going to offer?"

Abraham answered, "God will give us the lamb for sacrifice, my son."

When they arrived, Abraham built an altar and arranged the wood on it. Then he tied Isaac up and laid him on the wood. He raised the knife to kill Isaac, but at the last moment the Angel of the Lord said, "No! Don't hurt your son. I can see that you really do love and trust me. You were even willing to give me your precious son of promise."

Just then Abraham saw a ram caught in a bush nearby. He sacrificed the ram to God and named that place "The Lord Will Provide". They returned home. Abraham had passed God's test, and Isaac was spared.

——— 24 ———
Isaac Needs a Wife

Genesis 24

Sarah died several years after Isaac was born. Abraham and Isaac missed her very much. Isaac was now a grown man and was thinking about getting married. Abraham didn't want him to marry one of the women who lived in Canaan because they didn't love and worship God. So he decided to send his oldest, most trusted servant to look for a wife for Isaac. Abraham had many relatives where he used to live, and among them would be the right wife for his son.

The servant said, "If the woman won't come here, shall I take Isaac back there to marry her?"

"No!" Abraham answered. "God told me that this is where we should live, and Isaac must stay here. If she won't come, I will forgive you for being unable to keep the oath you are making. But please try to bring back a good wife for Isaac."

The servant promised to follow Abraham's instructions. He took many fine gifts with him and set out for the place where Abraham's relatives lived.

——— 25 ———
The Right Wife for Isaac

Genesis 24

The servant arrived at Nahor's village and stopped near a well. As he watched the women come to draw up water, he asked God to help him find a good wife for Isaac. He decided on a test. He would ask one of them to give him a drink of water. If she said yes and offered to water the camels, too, she would be the right one.

A beautiful young woman came to the well and filled her water pitcher. Abraham's servant asked her, "May I please have a drink?"

"Yes, sir. And I will be glad to draw water for your camels, too." And she kept drawing up water until the camels had had enough.

She had passed his test, so the servant offered her some of the gifts he had brought and asked her who she was. Her name was Rebekah. She was the daughter of Bethuel, a son of Nahor, which meant she was Abraham's grandniece and Isaac's cousin! The servant asked if he might stay overnight at her home because he wanted to ask her family to let her marry Isaac. Then he thanked God for helping him find Rebekah.

26

God Answers a Prayer

Genesis 24

Rebekah hurried home to tell her family about the man at the well. Her brother, Laban, invited the visitor to their home, and the servant told them his story.

They listened, amazed, when he said he was their uncle Abraham's servant from Canaan. He told them he had prayed that God would lead him to the right wife for Isaac. He said he had tested Rebekah, and she was the one he was looking for.

Rebekah's father and brother said, "We can see that God brought you here. You may take Rebekah to be Isaac's wife."

The servant thanked God. Then he gave Rebekah and her family the rest of the gifts. He wanted to leave the next morning, but her mother and brother, Laban, said, "We want her to stay with us a few more days. But we'll ask her what she wants to do." Rebekah said she would go at once, so her family gave her their blessing. When they got to Canaan, the servant told Isaac the story of how he had found Rebekah. Rebekah became Isaac's bride, and he loved her very much.

27

Esau Throws Away Something Valuable

Genesis 25

Rebekah had twin baby boys, Esau and Jacob. Esau was the older one, so he received the birthright. That meant that when his father died, Esau would receive most of the family money and land. The younger twin, Jacob, would get only half as much.

When they grew up, Esau became a skilful hunter. He would kill wild deer for food. Isaac liked that deer meat, called venison. He especially loved Esau. Jacob was quieter and preferred to stay at home. He was Rebekah's favourite son.

One day Jacob was cooking a big pot of stew. Esau came in from hunting, tired and hungry. He said, "Let me have some of that. It smells good."

Jacob saw a chance to cheat Esau. "All right, I will if you give me your birthright."

Esau said, "The birthright won't do me much good if I starve to death! You may have it." So Esau had a good supper. He was so hungry he didn't even care that he had traded something of great value for just a bowl of stew.

28

Jacob Fools His Father

Genesis 27

Isaac was getting old, and he was almost blind. He asked Esau to go hunting and bring back a deer. "Cook the meat the way I like it, and I will ask God to bless you."

Rebekah heard Isaac say this. She wanted Jacob to receive Isaac's blessing, so she thought of a way Jacob could trick Isaac. She cooked two young goats so that they tasted just like venison. When they were ready, she told Jacob to take them to his father.

"But Esau has a lot of hair on his arms and chest, and I don't. Father will know I'm not Esau."

So Rebekah tied some of the goatskin around Jacob. He took the meat to his father.

Isaac said, "Your voice sounds like Jacob's. Let me feel you to be sure you are Esau." He felt the goatskins on Jacob's arms and was satisfied. He ate the food and gave Jacob the blessing he had promised Esau.

When Esau came back and cooked the venison for his father, Isaac realized that Jacob had tricked him. It was too late. He had already given Jacob the special blessing.

29
Rebekah Helps Jacob Escape

Genesis 27

Esau saw how much he had lost through his own thoughtlessness and Jacob's trickery. He was furious with Jacob. "He got my birthright," he growled, "and now he has stolen my blessing. As soon as our father dies, I'm going to kill him."

Rebekah heard about Esau's threat. She told Jacob, "Your brother hates you. Go to Haran and stay with my brother, Laban, until Esau cools down. I will let you know when it is safe to return."

Esau was married to two Canaanite women who didn't love God, and this made his parents very unhappy. To get Isaac to let Jacob go to Haran, Rebekah said, "We don't want Jacob to marry one of the girls around here like Esau did, do we?"

Isaac agreed. He told Jacob to go to his grandfather Bethuel's home and find a good wife among Rebekah's relatives. This was just what Rebekah had wanted him to say. Isaac blessed Jacob and told him he would someday inherit the Land of Promise, as God had promised Abraham and Isaac before him.

Then Jacob quickly packed up and left.

30
A Stairway to Heaven

Genesis 28

Jacob travelled toward Haran. That night he slept on the ground with a stone for a pillow. He dreamt of a stairway reaching from earth to heaven. Angels were walking up and down it.

Then he saw the Lord, who said, "I am the God of Abraham and Isaac. You will be a part of the great nation I promised them. You will have many children, and this land will be yours forever. I will take care of you wherever you go. One day I will bring you back to this land. I'll never leave you."

Jacob woke up excited and afraid because God had come to him in a dream. He got up and worshipped God at an altar he made by setting up the stone he had used as a pillow. He poured oil over it as an offering. Jacob named that place Bethel, which means "the house of God".

Then Jacob made a very serious promise. He promised that if God took care of him and brought him back to the Promised Land, he would always love and trust God. "I will worship you and give you one-tenth of everything you give me."

31
Jacob Marries Leah and Rachel

Genesis 29

When Jacob got to where his mother's relatives lived, he met his cousin Rachel at the well. She was Laban's younger daughter. Jacob helped her water her sheep.

Then he told her who he was. She told her father, and Laban welcomed Jacob.

Jacob stayed with Laban's family and helped with his sheep. After about a month, Laban said, "You shouldn't work for nothing. Tell me what payment you want."

Jacob was in love with Rachel. He told Laban he would work for him free for seven years if Laban would let him marry Rachel. Laban agreed. After seven years, it was time for the wedding.

When the wedding feast was over, Laban brought Jacob's bride to his tent after dark. When he woke up in the morning, Jacob found that Laban had tricked him and given him Rachel's older sister, Leah, whom he didn't love. He was angry, so Laban said, "It was important that the older girl be married first. You may have Rachel, too, if you will work for another seven years." Jacob agreed.

32
Jacob's Secret Escape

Genesis 29–31

Leah's servant girl was called Zilpah, and Rachel's, Bilhah. Jacob married both of them, too. His four wives bore him many sons, but his favourite was Rachel's son Joseph. Jacob wanted to go back to Canaan, but Laban didn't want him to leave. Jacob said, "I'll stay if you will give me some sheep and goats so I can have flocks of my own."

Laban agreed, and soon Jacob's flocks grew very large, making him a rich man. Laban's sons became jealous of Jacob and his wealth. Jacob realized he would have to leave Haran secretly. He and his wives took all Jacob's flocks and everything they owned and left very quietly one day when Laban was out shearing his sheep.

Three days went by before Laban knew they were gone. He followed Jacob, and when he caught up with them, he said he just wanted to say goodbye to his daughters and his grandchildren. They camped together overnight, then said goodbye. On the way to Canaan, Jacob saw some angels, so he knew God was with him.

33
Jacob Wants Peace with Esau

Genesis 32

Jacob wondered how Esau would feel about his coming back. It had been twenty years since Jacob had tricked Isaac and stolen Esau's blessing. Was Esau still angry with him? Did he still want to kill him? Jacob decided to send messengers to Esau to tell him he was coming and that he wanted to be friends.

The messengers came back and said, "Esau is coming out to meet you, and he has four hundred men with him." That really scared Jacob! He divided his family, servants, and flocks into two groups. If Esau should attack, at least one group might be able to escape. Next, Jacob prayed that God would protect him from Esau's anger. He thanked God for all the good things that had happened to him in Haran.

Then Jacob gathered several hundred of his animals as a gift for Esau. He sent servants ahead with the animals to meet his brother. He thought it might make Esau less angry with him. Maybe they would be able to be friends after all.

34
Jacob Prepares to Meet Esau

Genesis 32

Jacob wanted to protect his wives and children in case there was fighting when he met Esau. So for safety, he sent them across the River Jordan. When he returned to his camp, a man came and started wrestling with him. They wrestled until early morning. When the man saw that he could not overcome Jacob, he put Jacob's hip out of joint.

The man said, "It is morning; let me go now."

Jacob answered, "No, not until you bless me."

"What is your name?" the man asked.

Jacob told him.

"I'm going to change your name to Israel, which means 'one who struggles and prevails with God.' You will also be strong and prevail with men."

Jacob asked the man his name. The man would not tell him, but he gave Jacob the blessing he had asked for. Jacob knew then that the man was the Lord in the form of a man. Jacob named the place where they had wrestled Peniel, which means "the face of God". He said, "I saw God face-to-face, and yet my life was spared."

35
God Cares for Jacob

Genesis 33

The moment came for Jacob and Esau to meet. Jacob went on ahead of his family, and as he came close to Esau, he bowed down to show his respect. Esau ran to meet him and hugged and kissed him. They were so glad to see each other that they both cried for joy.

When Esau saw Jacob's large family, he asked, "Who are all these women and children with you?"

Jacob replied, "These are the children God has given me."

Esau asked, "And why did you send all those animals to me?"

Jacob said, "I sent them as a gift – to make you feel friendly toward me."

Esau said, "I have all the flocks and herds I need. You keep them." But Jacob insisted, and finally Esau accepted them.

Esau offered to travel with Jacob the rest of the way, but Jacob was still a little afraid of him. He told Esau to go on ahead and he and his family would follow more slowly.

So God answered Jacob's prayer and reunited him with Esau, and the brothers could be friends after twenty years apart.

36
The Death of Isaac

Genesis 33–35

Jacob travelled toward Canaan. He camped at Succoth, then entered Canaan and stayed at a city called Shechem. He bought a piece of land and built an altar. He called it "God, the God of Israel".

Then God sent him to Bethel to build an altar. Jacob knew Bethel well because he had dreamed about the stairway to heaven there and God had promised to bring him back safely.

Jacob built a great altar and made sacrifices to show God how grateful he was for his blessings. God reminded him about his new name, "Israel", and about the great nation he had promised Abraham.

On the way to Bethlehem, Rachel had another baby boy, Benjamin. After the baby was born, Rachel died. Jacob was terribly sad because he had loved her so much. He went on to see his father, Isaac, who was now very, very old. When Isaac died, Jacob and Esau buried him where Abraham and Sarah were buried.

Esau took his family and moved to Edom, where his flocks would have more pasture. Jacob and his twelve sons stayed in the Promised Land.

37
Joseph the Dreamer

Genesis 37

Because Jacob had loved Rachel best, her son Joseph was his favourite child. Jacob gave Joseph special privileges and gifts, like a beautiful colourful robe. This made the other sons angry and jealous of Joseph.

One day, when Joseph was seventeen years old, he told his brothers about a dream he had had in which their bundles of grain bowed down to his bundle of grain. It made the brothers angry. "If you think we would ever bow down to you, you can forget it!" they growled.

Now they hated Joseph even more.

Later Joseph had another dream, which he described to his family. "I dreamed that the sun and the moon and eleven stars were bowing down to me," he said. Jacob scolded him. "Do you think your mother and I and your brothers will actually come and bow to you?"

Joseph's older brothers continued to be jealous and hateful toward him. Jacob thought a lot about Joseph's strange dreams and wondered why his son dreamed such things.

38
Joseph Visits His Brothers

Genesis 37

Jacob's sons took care of all his flocks and herds. One day they took the animals to Shechem to find good pasture. Jacob sent Joseph to find them and bring back news about them. Joseph wandered around the fields, hunting for them, but he couldn't find them.

He met a man who said, "Jacob's sons? I heard them say they were going to Dothan." So Joseph followed them to Dothan.

When his brothers saw him in the distance, they groaned. "Look who's coming. It's the dreamer! Let's get rid of him for good. We'll kill him and toss him into a well and tell Father that a wild animal ate him."

The oldest brother, Reuben, didn't like the idea of killing his young brother. He said, "Let's put him into a dry well. Maybe he'll die in there without our having to hurt him ourselves." Reuben thought that later he could secretly rescue Joseph.

When Joseph arrived, his brothers grabbed his colourful coat. They threw him into an empty well – and then sat down to eat their lunch.

39
Joseph's Brothers Get Rid of Him

Genesis 37

While Reuben was busy elsewhere, a caravan of camels came by. Some Ishmaelites were going to Egypt. Judah had an idea. "Listen," he said, "instead of killing Joseph, let's sell him to these traders. They will pay us and take him away so he can't bother us anymore."

So they pulled Joseph out of the well and sold him to the traders for twenty pieces of silver. The traders went on toward Egypt. Soon Reuben came back to camp and looked for Joseph, but he was gone. Reuben was terribly upset. "What are we going to tell our father?

He will be broken-hearted if Joseph doesn't return with us."

They decided to let Jacob think Joseph had been killed by a wild animal. They killed a goat and put a lot of its blood on Joseph's beautiful coat. They returned to Jacob and said, "We found this robe on the ground."

"It's Joseph's coat. He must have been attacked by a wild beast and torn to bits. My dear son is dead!" Day after day Jacob grieved for Joseph. He said, "I will be sad about his death all the rest of my life."

40
Joseph Goes to Jail

Genesis 39–40

The traders took Joseph to Egypt
and sold him to Potiphar, an officer
in the king's army. In Egypt the kings
were called "Pharaoh". Potiphar was
the captain of Pharaoh's bodyguards.
Joseph worked in Potiphar's home, and
he did so well that Potiphar trusted him
with more and more important jobs.

But Potiphar's wife liked Joseph too
much. She tried to get Joseph to make
love to her. Joseph knew this was very
wrong, so he refused. She was furious
and told lies about Joseph to get him
into trouble. Potiphar believed her lies
and threw Joseph into prison.

Joseph worked so well in prison that
the chief jailer put him in charge of the
other prisoners.

Pharaoh's baker and butler, the man
who served his wine, were in the same
jail as Joseph.

One night these men had strange
dreams, and Joseph was able to tell them
what their dreams meant. The baker was
executed, but the butler was allowed to
go back to the palace, just as Joseph had
said. Joseph said to the butler, "When
you get out of prison, please ask the
king to let me out too." Unfortunately,
the man forgot all about Joseph.

41
Pharaoh's Dreams

Genesis 41

Two years passed, and still Joseph was
in prison. One night Pharaoh had a
dream. He saw seven fat cows come
out of the Nile River. Then seven thin
cows came and ate up the fat ones. The
king woke up, then fell asleep again
and had another dream. This time he
saw seven good ears of corn growing
on a cornstalk. Then seven withered
ears appeared and ate up the good ears.
Pharaoh woke up worried.

He asked his
wisest men what
the dreams
meant, but
they didn't

know. Then the butler remembered Joseph and said, "When I was in prison, I knew a man who could tell what dreams meant."

Pharaoh sent for Joseph immediately and told him his dreams. He asked Joseph what they meant. Joseph said, "I don't interpret dreams by myself; my God helps me understand them." Then Joseph said the dreams meant there would be seven good years, with plenty of food, followed by seven bad years, when the crops wouldn't grow.

Joseph suggested that the king put someone in charge of storing up corn during the good years so there would be enough to eat during the bad years. The king said, "Good! You are the right person for the job!"

42
Jacob's Sons Buy Grain
Genesis 41–42

Pharaoh made Joseph a great leader in Egypt. During the seven good years, Joseph made every farmer give some grain to the king. Joseph stored the extra grain in big buildings in the cities.

When the seven years of famine came, crops wouldn't grow. The farmers had nothing to feed their animals or their families. The people begged their king to help them. Pharaoh said, "I put Joseph in charge of famine relief. Ask him what to do." When the hungry people came to Joseph, he opened the barns and sold grain to them. They and their animals had enough to eat.

The famine was bad in Canaan, too. Jacob's family desperately needed grain. Jacob said to his sons, "I have heard there is plenty of grain in Egypt. Go and buy some for us, or we will starve." So all ten of Joseph's elder brothers set off for Egypt.

When they got there, they asked where they could buy grain. "Go and see our governor," was the answer. "He is in charge of supplies."

43
Joseph's Brothers Don't Recognize Him

Genesis 42

When Jacob's sons found the governor, they didn't recognize him as their brother. He had grown older and had changed a lot. Also, he was wearing Egyptian clothes and was an important government official. Joseph recognized them right away, but he pretended he didn't know them. They all bowed low to Joseph, just as in his dreams.

They told Joseph they had come from Canaan and needed to buy food for their families.

"No, you are spies who have come to see how bad our famine is so you can bring an army against us," said Joseph, pretending to be very angry.

"Oh, no. We are not spies. We are Jacob's sons, and we have another brother at home. There used to be twelve of us, but one brother died."

Joseph kept on pretending not to recognize them. He said, "I can find out if you're telling the truth. I'll put you in jail; then I'll send one of you back to get your youngest brother." So he put them in jail for three days.

44

Joseph Sends for His Favourite Brother

Genesis 42

After three days, Joseph let his brothers out of jail. "I'll keep just one of you in jail," he said, "and the rest shall return home with enough grain to keep your families from starving. But you must bring your youngest brother back here to me, so I'll know you have been truthful with me."

The men agreed to do this. They talked among themselves about the trouble they were having. "This is God's way of punishing us for the terrible thing we did to our brother Joseph," they said.

Reuben said, "Remember how I told you not to harm the boy – but you wouldn't listen to me. Now see what a mess we're in!"

They didn't realize that Joseph could understand what they were saying. When he heard they were sorry about

the way they had treated him, he had to hide his tears. Then he told them he would keep Simeon as his prisoner until they brought their young brother from Canaan.

Benjamin was Joseph's favourite brother. He was Joseph's full brother instead of a half-brother like the rest of the men, who had different mothers.

45

Joseph Sees Benjamin

Genesis 43

Joseph's servant loaded bags of grain onto the brothers' donkeys. He told the servant to hide the money his brothers had paid him in the bags. The brothers started home. That night when they opened a bag to get some grain to eat, there was their money! This scared them because they didn't know how it had got there. When they got home and unloaded the grain, they found money in every bag. It was frightening. They told Jacob that the governor of Egypt would not let Simeon go unless they returned with Benjamin. Jacob said, "No! I lost Joseph, and now Simeon is gone. You can't take Benjamin, too."

Soon their grain was gone. Jacob told his sons to go back and buy some more. Judah said, "Father, we can't unless we take Benjamin. Please let him go. I will look after him." Finally Jacob agreed. When Joseph saw Benjamin he was so happy that, in private, he cried for joy. He invited his brothers to a dinner and seated them according to their ages. They wondered how he knew so much about them. Joseph gave Benjamin five times as much food as the others!

46
The Cup in the Sack

Genesis 44

Joseph asked his brothers whether their father was still alive. He was happy when they told him that Jacob was well. Joseph's servant filled the men's bags with grain. As before, Joseph told him to put their money in the bags. Then he said, "Put my silver cup in the youngest brother's bag, along with his money."

The next morning the brothers started for home. Soon afterward, Joseph sent the servant after them to accuse them of stealing the silver cup. "We wouldn't think of doing such a thing," they said. "Search us. If you find it, we'll kill whoever stole it and the rest of us will go back and be the governor's slaves."

The servant said, "No, only the one who stole it will have to be a slave. The rest of you may go home." He searched through all the bags of grain, beginning with the oldest brother's and working his way down to Benjamin's. And there it was in Benjamin's

bag! They were all shocked. They rode back into the city with the servant and hurried to see Joseph.

47
A Surprising Announcement
Genesis 44–45

When Joseph saw his brothers, he pretended that he thought Benjamin had stolen his silver cup. Judah spoke for everyone. "We are innocent, but we can't prove it. This is a punishment for our past sins. We will all be your slaves."

"I want only the one who had the cup in his bag."

"Sir, we can't do that! Our elderly father has lost the son he loved best. If we go back without his youngest son, he will die of grief. Please let the boy go home with my other brothers. I will take his place and be your slave forever."

Joseph saw how kind his brothers had become and how much they cared about their father. He couldn't keep up the pretence. He sent all his servants away and started to cry.

Then he said, "I am your brother Joseph! God spared me so I could save you from dying in the famine. I really am Joseph. Go back and tell my father I'm all right. Bring him here quickly because the famine is going to last another five years."

At first his brothers couldn't believe it, but finally they recognized him, and they were so happy!

48
Jacob Moves to Egypt
Genesis 45–46

Pharaoh heard that Joseph's brothers were there. He told them to take plenty of grain back to their father and said, "Bring Jacob and your families to Egypt to live. I'll give you the best land in the whole country."

Joseph sent his brothers back with grain and many gifts for everyone. Benjamin was given more than anybody else. The brothers returned to Jacob and told him that Joseph was alive and was a great ruler in Egypt. At first Jacob couldn't believe it. But when he saw Joseph's gifts and heard about Joseph's life in Egypt, he began to realize it was true!

They packed up and set out for Egypt. Along the way God spoke to Jacob, "Don't be afraid to go to Egypt. This is part of my plan. I'll be with you,

and I will bring you back home again. And when you die, Joseph will be with you."

Because Jacob's new name was Israel, the Bible calls his family and descendants "Israelites". Another name for them is "Jews". Jacob and sixty-six Israelites travelled from Canaan to Egypt. Joseph and his two sons made a total of seventy.

49
A Happy Family Reunion

Genesis 46–47

When Jacob and his family got as far as Goshen, he sent Judah on ahead to let Joseph know they were coming. Joseph hurried out to meet them. Joseph and his father hugged each other and cried for a long time. Jacob said, "Now I will be able to die happy because I have seen you again!"

Joseph introduced five of his brothers to Pharaoh. "My brothers are shepherds, and they have brought many flocks and herds from Canaan."

The brothers asked the king, "May we live in Goshen, where our flocks will have plenty to eat?" They wanted to live in Goshen because people in most parts of Egypt didn't like shepherds and wouldn't welcome them.

Pharaoh said, "Yes, if Goshen is where you want to live, you are welcome to make your home there. If you are especially good shepherds, you can take care of my flocks, too." Then Joseph presented his father to the king. Pharaoh welcomed him kindly, and Jacob gave Pharaoh a special blessing.

So that is how Jacob's family got settled in Egypt.

50
A Blessing for Each Son

Genesis 48–50

Jacob lived in Egypt for seventeen years. Then he became very ill. Joseph took his two sons, Manasseh and Ephraim, to see their grandfather. Jacob blessed his grandsons.

He surprised Joseph by saying that the younger boy would be greater than the older one.

Then Jacob called all of his sons to come and receive his blessing: Leah's sons – Reuben, Simeon, Levi, Judah, Issachar, and Zebulun; Bilhah the slave-wife's sons – Dan and Naphtali; Zilpah the slave-wife's sons – Gad and Asher; Rachel's sons – Joseph and Benjamin.

Finally Jacob asked his sons to bury him in the family burial cave in Canaan. Then he lay down and died. Joseph was very sad. Pharaoh gave him permission to take Jacob's body to Canaan.

Joseph's brothers thought Joseph

might turn against them now that Jacob was no longer alive. But Joseph said, "You thought you were harming me when I was a boy, but God turned that harm into good for all of us."

Joseph lived in Egypt all the rest of his life. When he died, he asked that his bones be taken back to Canaan. Four hundred years went by before that happened.

— 51 —
The Cruel Egyptians

Exodus 1

After Jacob and Joseph had both died, their families kept growing. Many years went by, and their children, grandchildren, and great-grandchildren were so many that it was almost impossible to count them. That is what God had said would happen when he had promised Abraham that his descendants would become a great nation.

After several hundred years, a pharaoh was ruling who didn't know anything about Joseph. This new pharaoh was worried about what a large nation the people of Israel had become. He thought they might become so powerful that they would turn against Egypt and help Egypt's enemies.

He also worried that they might decide to return to where they had come from and he would not have them to work for him anymore. So he ordered all the Egyptians to make the Israelites their slaves.

The Egyptians treated the people of Israel cruelly and made them work very hard. Because the Israelites were slaves, they were prisoners in Egypt. But God had promised to take care of them, and he always keeps his promises. More Israelite children were born, and the nation continued to grow.

52
The Baby in the Floating Basket

Exodus 1–2

When Pharaoh saw how the Israelite families were growing, he ordered the midwives, who helped the Israelite mothers when they were giving birth, to kill the baby boys as soon as they were born. The midwives knew this was wrong, so they disobeyed Pharaoh, and God blessed them because of it. Then Pharaoh told his own people to take the baby boys away from the Israelites and throw them into the Nile River.

A man and his wife, of the family of Levi, had a baby boy – their third child. They loved their little son, so they hid him, hoping no Egyptian would find him and kill him. When the baby was three months old, he was getting too big to hide.

His mother decided to weave a basket and make it waterproof by coating it with tar. Then she put her baby boy into the basket and hid it among the tall grasses at the edge of the river. The baby's older sister, Miriam, hid nearby to watch the basket and see what would happen to her baby brother.

53
A Princess Finds a Surprise

Exodus 2

Pharaoh had a daughter who went to bathe in the Nile River. As she was walking along the riverbank, the princess noticed the basket floating among the reeds. She sent one of her maids to pick it up out of the water and bring it to her.

When she looked inside, she was amazed to see a beautiful baby boy! The baby began to cry. The princess felt sorry for him and wanted to keep him safe. "I'm going to adopt this baby as my own," she said.

Just then Miriam, the baby's sister, came out from her hiding place. She asked the princess, "Would you like me to get one of the Jewish women to nurse him while he is so small?"

Pharaoh's daughter said, "Yes, please." So Miriam went home and got her mother.

The princess said, "Take this baby home, and nurse him for me. I'll pay you for taking care of him."

So the baby's mother took care of her own little boy until he was old enough to go to live with the princess and be her adopted son. The princess named the little boy Moses.

54

Moses Escapes

Exodus 2

Although Moses grew up in the royal family, he never forgot that he was one of the people of Israel.

One day he saw an Egyptian hitting one of his Israelite relatives. This made Moses terribly angry. He made sure no one was watching; then he killed the Egyptian and buried his body in the sand.

The next day he saw two Israelite men fighting. He said to the one who was in the wrong, "Why are you hitting your own Israelite brother?"

The man answered him angrily, "That's none of your business! You're not my judge. Do you plan to kill me the way you killed that Egyptian yesterday?"

Moses realized that someone had seen his crime and that he was in trouble. Sure enough, Pharaoh tried to find Moses so he could arrest him and execute him for murder. But Moses escaped. He fled to Midian. There he saw some men being unkind to several sisters who wanted to water their father's sheep at a well. Moses helped the sisters. Their father, Reuel, was grateful, so he hired Moses to work as a shepherd and later let Moses marry his daughter Zipporah.

----------- 55 -----------
The Bush That Kept Burning

Exodus 3

While Moses was in Midian, the people of Israel were suffering in Egypt. They cried out to God for help, and he heard them. It was time to rescue his people. One day Moses was out tending his father-in-law's sheep. Suddenly he noticed something strange. A bush was on fire, but it wasn't burning up. He went closer. Then he heard a voice speaking to him.

"Moses!" the voice said. "I am God.

Don't come any closer. Take off your shoes because this is holy ground." Moses was afraid to look at God, so he covered his face.

"I have heard my people in Egypt crying for help," God said. "I have chosen you to go to Pharaoh and tell him to let my people go. You are to lead them back to the Land of Promise."

"No!" Moses replied. "I could never do that."

"You can do it because I will be with you," God said.

Moses said, "If I tell the people you have sent me, they will ask, 'What is the name of this God?' What shall I say?"

God answered, "Tell them that 'I AM' has sent you."

56
Moses Can Do Miracles

Exodus 4

Although God promised Moses he would help him, Moses was still afraid. He thought the people wouldn't believe that God had talked to him. And Pharaoh would not want to let the slave-nation of Israel leave Egypt.

Finally God showed Moses how powerful he was. God told Moses to throw his shepherd's rod down on the ground. Moses obeyed, and immediately the rod turned into a live snake. Moses jumped away from it. Then God said to him, "Grab the snake by the tail."

Carefully Moses picked up the snake. Immediately it turned into a rod again. God said, "When you do that miracle, the people will believe I sent you. Now put your hand inside your robe, next to your chest."

When Moses did this and took his hand out again, it was covered with the disease leprosy.

"Do it again," God ordered. Moses did, and this time the leprosy was gone and his skin was healthy. "If the people don't believe the first miracle, they may believe the second – then they will listen to you."

57
Aaron Will Help His Brother

Exodus 4

God told Moses another way that he could prove he was God's messenger. He could take some water from the Nile River and pour it on the ground, and it would turn into blood. But Moses was still afraid and made another excuse. He said, "O Lord, I'm not a powerful speaker."

God said, "I can make you a good speaker, if you will only trust me." But Moses still didn't want to go. He said, "No, Lord. Find someone else to do this job."

God became angry with him. He said, "All right, I'll send your brother, Aaron, with you. He can speak for you. You tell him what to say, and he will deliver the messages. But I am going to give you the ability to talk well, too. Now take your shepherd's rod and go!"

Moses got his father-in-law's permission to leave. He took his wife and sons and started the trip. Before he left, God said, "The Pharaoh who wanted to kill you has died. Don't be afraid to go because no one in Egypt wants to hurt you anymore."

58
Pharaoh's Hard Heart

Exodus 4–5

God told Aaron to meet Moses at Mount Horeb. Moses told Aaron what God wanted them to do, and about the miraculous signs. They gave God's message to the leaders of the people of Israel, and Moses showed them the wonderful miracles. The elders of Israel believed that God had sent Moses and Aaron. They were very thankful that God had not forgotten them, and they worshipped the Lord.

Then Moses and Aaron went to tell Pharaoh what God had said. They said, "The Lord God of Israel has sent us to you with this message: 'Let my people go out into the desert to worship me.'"

Pharaoh was unimpressed. He said, "Who is this God, and why should I pay any attention to him? I refuse to let the Israelites stop work to make a trip. Now get out!" Then he ordered the supervisors to make the slaves work harder than ever. He said, "Don't give them any more straw. They must make as many bricks as before, but they must find their own straw. They'll be so busy they won't have time to think about trips to the desert!"

— 59 —
The People Complain to Moses

Exodus 5–7

The Israelite slaves suffered greatly as they had to work harder and harder. If they slowed down, the masters beat them and said they were lazy. The slaves blamed Moses and Aaron. "Everything is much worse for us since you asked Pharaoh to let us go," they said angrily. "You've made Pharaoh hate us. If he kills us, it will be your fault!"

Moses talked to God about this. "I thought you were going to rescue your people," he said. "But they are in worse trouble than before."

The Lord told Moses to be patient. He would see how well God would take care of the Israelites. God said, "Tell the people not to give up hope." Then he said they should try again with Pharaoh.

So Moses went back to Pharaoh and again asked him to release the slaves. This time Aaron threw down his rod and it became a snake. But Pharaoh's magicians were able to do the same miracle.

Then something exciting happened: Aaron's snake swallowed up all the magicians' snakes! Still Pharaoh was too stubborn to let the slaves go.

60
Big Trouble for Egypt

Exodus 7–8

Again God told Moses to speak to Pharaoh, so Moses met Pharaoh the next morning by the river. Moses repeated his message from God, but Pharaoh said no. Then the Lord told Aaron to point his rod over the river. Aaron did this and then struck the water. At that very moment all the water in the river – and all the other water in Egypt – changed into blood.

The fish all died, and the people of Egypt had no clean water to drink. This went on for seven days, but Pharaoh still refused to let the people go.

The next week Aaron pointed his rod again, and thousands of frogs appeared. They filled the whole country. They were everywhere! Pharaoh

begged Moses and Aaron to get rid of the frogs. "If you do," he said, "I will let the people go to the desert."

"When shall I do this?" Moses asked.

"Tomorrow," Pharaoh answered.

So the next day all the frogs died. But Pharaoh changed his mind and broke his promise to Moses.

61
Frightening Punishments

Exodus 8–10

God kept giving Pharaoh chances to let the people go. Each time, Pharaoh said he would; then at the last moment he would break his word. God made the dust turn into insects called gnats, which made life miserable. Then swarms of flies came down upon the Egyptians. The next punishment was a disease that killed the animals.

Then awful sores called boils broke out all over people's skin. Next God sent a violent storm that destroyed the crops and hurt the Egyptians.

Pharaoh tried to make a deal with Moses to let only the men go but Moses wouldn't agree. This time God sent a great swarm of locusts that ate up every plant, tree, and blade of grass. Pharaoh said he would let the people go if Moses got rid of the locusts. But he didn't keep that promise either.

Next God sent a thick darkness over Egypt. For three days people were afraid to move because they couldn't see a thing. Pharaoh said, "Take the people, but leave the animals behind." But Moses said that wasn't what God had told them to do. So again Pharaoh refused to let them go.

come in the middle of the night, and the firstborn son in every home will die. Your own son will die, Pharaoh, along with all the other firstborn. Every Egyptian family will be in deep sorrow. But no Israelite child shall die. The Israelites are very special to God, and he will take care of them. You will beg us to leave the country. Then I will take my people and go."

Moses turned and hurried out of the palace. He already knew that Pharaoh would not listen to him. God had hardened the king's heart so he could show everyone his own power and glory.

62
The Worst Punishment

Exodus 11

Finally God said to Moses, "I'm going to send one final, dreadful punishment. When it is over, Pharaoh will beg you to take my people and go. But first, tell my people to ask their Egyptian friends and neighbours to give them pieces of gold and silver jewellery."

So Moses went to Pharaoh one more time and said, "God is going to

63
The First Passover

Exodus 12

Moses and Aaron's next job was to tell the people of Israel what God wanted them to do. They had to get ready for the night when God would visit the homes of the Egyptians and kill the firstborn sons. Here are the instructions God gave them:
1. Each family should kill a perfect one-year-old lamb or baby goat.

2. They should use a certain weed as a brush and paint some of the lamb's blood on each side and over the top of their front door.

3. Then they should roast the lamb and eat it, along with the bitter-tasting herbs and hard bread made without yeast.

4. They must eat all of it that night and not save any for the next day.

5. While they eat it, they are to wear their travelling clothes and their sandals and carry a walking stick.

Then God made a wonderful promise to his people. He said, "When I go through the land, killing the firstborn of the Egyptians, I will see the blood on your doors. That will show me that you have obeyed my instructions, and I will pass over your homes and not kill your firstborn sons." He said that from then on, they were to have this ceremony on a certain day every year in memory of his goodness to them. The annual celebration should be called "the Lord's Passover", because he had passed over their homes when he saw the blood on the doors.

64
Pharaoh Lets the People Go
Exodus 12

The people of Israel followed God's instructions. At midnight the Lord passed through the nation of Egypt, and the firstborn in every family died. Even the firstborn cattle died. All the Egyptian people got up in the middle of the night to see what had happened. They were all heartbroken to find that in every Egyptian home someone had died.

Pharaoh knew this tragedy had happened because he had not listened to the warnings of Moses and Aaron. Quickly he called them to his court and said, "Hurry and leave my country! Take your families and your flocks and herds of animals. Get out quickly, and worship your God any way you want to. But before you go, please bless me." The Israelites asked their Egyptian friends and neighbours for gold and silver jewellery, and the Egyptians gladly gave it to them. Then the people of Israel packed up all their things and set out – 600,000 men, plus all the women and children.

65
A Path through the Sea
Exodus 14

Led by Moses and Aaron, the people of Israel started their long journey back to Canaan, the Land of Promise. The Lord told Moses to camp by the sea. He said, "Pharaoh is going to change his mind again and chase your people. I will

protect you from Pharaoh's army as it chases you." Moses obeyed.

When Pharaoh heard that the people of Israel had left and did not intend to return, he was sorry he had let them go. He said, "We have let a lot of valuable workers get away. We must get them back." He called together his army and chased the Israelites.

When the people saw the Egyptians coming, they were angry with Moses for putting them in danger. But Moses said, "Don't worry; God will rescue us." And he stood by the sea and raised his rod over the water. Then God divided the water, opening up a path right through the sea.

God surrounded the Israelites with a cloud so Pharaoh's soldiers couldn't find them. The people of Israel escaped by walking across the sea on the dry path God had made.

66
Pharaoh's Soldiers Drown

Exodus 14–15

Pharaoh's huge army was not far behind the people of Israel. The soldiers were able to see the path on which the Israelites had started to cross the sea, so they followed them. The chariots and horsemen went between the great walls of water that were piled up on each side of the path. Then God slowed them down. Wheels started falling off their chariots. The soldiers became frightened because God was on the Israelites' side.

As soon as the last person in Moses' group was safely across the sea, God told Moses to raise his rod over the water again. The waters on each side came crashing down on the path. The whole Egyptian army drowned.

Then the people of Israel realized how good God had been to them. They had great love and respect for him and also for his servant Moses. Moses led them in singing a song of praise to the Lord.

— 67 —
Food from Heaven

Exodus 16

The people forgot how good God had been to them. They became thirsty, but the only water they could find was bitter. They complained to Moses, and he asked God what to do. God told him to throw a tree into the bitter water. Instantly the water became good to drink. Later, when they were hungry, they blamed Moses, saying, "At least we had enough to eat in Egypt."

God told Moses, "I am going to send food for all the people; then they will remember that I am the Lord their God."

That evening a large number of birds called quail flew into the camp, so the people had all the meat they could eat. The next morning, after the dew had dried up, the ground was covered with thin white flakes that looked a little like bread. The people called it manna.

The Lord told Moses, "Every morning each family should gather what they need for one day. Don't try to save it for the next day, or it will spoil. On the sixth day, pick up enough for two days, and it won't spoil. I won't send any food on the Sabbath because it is a special, holy day."

you. Then take your rod and hit the rock. Immediately, water will pour out." Moses did exactly what God told him to do, and water flowed from the rock. There was plenty for all the people to drink.

69
Joshua Leads the Army
Exodus 17

While the people were still at Rephidim, an army from Amalek attacked them. Moses chose a very brave man named Joshua to lead Israel's army. He said, "Joshua, choose the men you need, and go and fight the Amalekites. I will stand on a hill and watch. Aaron and Hur will be with me. I'll hold up my rod and point it out over the army. As long as I hold it there, God will give you and your soldiers victory."

While Moses held the rod

68
Water from a Rock
Exodus 17

The manna kept coming each morning, except on the Sabbath, all the time that the people of Israel were travelling on their way back to Canaan. When they came to Rephidim, near Mount Horeb, the people had no water left. They were getting very thirsty, but no one could find any water. They became angry with Moses and said, "It's all your fault. You took us away from Egypt and brought us to this desert place. Now we are all going to die without water."

Moses asked God what he should do. God told Moses to take the people to Mount Horeb. "Go to the rock I will show up, the people of Israel defeated the Amalekites. But sometimes his arms got so tired that he had to lower the rod. Then the Amalekites started to win the battle.

Aaron and Hur got a big rock for Moses to sit on. They stood, one on each side of Moses, and held up his arms so that the rod was always pointing out over the battlefield. Finally the battle was over, and the Israelite army had won.

God told Moses he would one day destroy all the people of Amalek. Then Moses built an altar and named it "The Lord is My Battle Flag".

70
God Calls Moses to the Mountain

Exodus 19

After the war with the Amalekites, the people of Israel continued to travel. They camped at Mount Sinai, where God told Moses to climb the mountain to talk with him. God said, "Tell the people how much I love them. I have rescued them from Egypt and have taken care of them. They will always be my special servants – a holy nation."

Moses gave the people God's message. They promised to obey God and be his special people. Then God told Moses that the people must prepare themselves for a time when God would send them important instructions and rules. They must get their hearts ready to hear what God would tell them. They would hear a trumpet call, and they would know that God was ready to speak to them through Moses. Only Moses was allowed to go up onto the mountain.

The trumpet sounded, and smoke rose from the mountain. All the people stood around the foot of it while Moses climbed up to meet God.

Commandments About Loving God

Exodus 20

God met Moses on Mount Sinai and told him how he wanted the people of Israel to live. He gave Moses ten important rules, the Ten commandments. The first four of those rules tell how people should feel about God himself.

1. **I am Jehovah your God. You shall not worship any other god.**
   Our God made us and loves us. He wants us to love and worship him. We must not believe in false gods.

2. **You shall not bow down and worship any kind of idol.**
   Each of us can begin to love something more than we love God. It might be money or clothes or special friends. These things can get to be like idols. God says to worship only him.

3. **You shall not take the name of God in vain.**
   When we use God's name, we should do it respectfully because he is a holy God. We must not swear or say God's name in an irreverent way.

4. **You shall keep the Sabbath as a holy day.**
   God created everything in six days, and on the seventh day he rested. He wants us to keep one day as a special day on which we worship him.

others and wishing they were dead is like having murder in our hearts.

7. **You shall not commit adultery.**
   This commandment is about sexual sin. If a man and a woman sleep together when they are not married to each other, that is adultery. We must also keep our thoughts and words pure.

8. **You shall not steal.**
   We must never take anything that belongs to someone else and keep it as our own.

9. **You shall not tell lies.**
   We must be very sure that everything we say is exactly true and that we don't hide the truth by keeping quiet when we should speak.

10. **You shall not covet anything that belongs to your neighbour.**
    Coveting is wishing we could have things that belong to other people. God wants us to be content with what he has given us.

72
Commandments About Loving Others

Exodus 20

The rest of the commandments tell us how we should behave toward other people.

5. **Honour your father and your mother.**
   We must respect our parents and obey them.

6. **You shall not commit murder.**
   Murder is always wrong. Hating

73
A Special House for God

Exodus 24–27

The people promised to obey God's rules. Then God called Moses back to the mountain so he could give him the Ten Commandments carved on pieces of stone. Moses took Joshua with him. God told Moses he wanted the people to build a special place in which to worship him. He described it to Moses very carefully. Because the people were travelling, it had to be easy to move, so

God said it must be a tent that could be carried. This building was to be called the tabernacle.

Then God described the furniture that should go into the tabernacle. One of the most important pieces would be the ark of the covenant, a beautiful chest made of wood and then covered with gold. The cover of the ark would be called the mercy seat. They were also to make a table, a lampstand with seven lamps, and altars on which offerings would be made and incense burned.

God told Moses to ask the people to provide the different materials as a gift to God. Moses would need gold, silver, bronze, beautiful cloth, wood, oil, spices, incense, and jewels.

74
Clothes for the Priests

Exodus 28

God appointed Aaron and his family to be in charge of the worship that would take place in the tabernacle. Aaron would be the high priest, and his four sons would help him. It would be the priests' job to sacrifice the animals the people brought as offerings to God.

God wanted the priests to have special clothing to show that they had been especially chosen for their work. Aaron would wear an embroidered robe covered by a blue coat. Around the hem of the coat would be bells and decorations in the shape of pomegranates. Over the coat he was to wear a cloth vest, called an ephod, which had twelve kinds of jewels sewn onto the front. Each jewel represented one of the tribes of Israel.

Aaron was to wear special shirts and undergarments. On his head he should wear a linen turban with a gold plate on the front of it, with the words "Holiness to the Lord". Aaron's sons were also to wear robes, sashes, and turbans. God told Moses to have a special dedication ceremony for the priests.

75
Dedicating the Priests

Exodus 29

God gave Moses more details about the dedication of Aaron and his sons. He was to prepare special bread and bring a young bull and two rams that were perfect. He was to have Aaron and his sons bathe at the entrance to the tabernacle, then dress them in the clothing God had described. He should pour oil on Aaron's head. This showed that a person was chosen to do a very special work for God.

Next they should offer first the young bull and then the rams to God. The meat and the bread were symbols, or signs, of obedience, setting Aaron and his sons apart from all the other people. They were priests in the house of God – the tabernacle.

This ceremony was to be repeated every day for seven days. As offerings were made on the altar, the altar was dedicated to God and became a holy place of offering and worship. God said that if these instructions were followed carefully, he would always live among the people of Israel and be the Lord their God.

76
A Gold Calf-Idol

Exodus 31–32

Moses was still on Mount Sinai. Finally, God gave him the tablets of stone on which God himself had written the Ten Commandments. The people had been waiting at the foot of the mountain for more than a month. They were becoming very impatient.

Some of them went to Aaron and said, "Something must have happened to Moses. Now we don't have anyone to tell us what God says. Please make us a new god to take care of us and lead us on our journey." They had already forgotten their promise not to worship any false god or idol.

Aaron was disobedient too. He agreed to do what they asked. He said, "Give me your gold jewellery." He melted it down and formed it into the shape of a calf. The people worshipped the calf-idol. They had a feast, got drunk, and broke another of God's commandments by committing sexual sins.

God was able to see everything. He told Moses, "Hurry down the mountain and see what your people are doing. They are worshipping an idol and are breaking many of my laws. I feel like destroying them because of their sin."

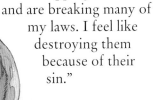

77
Moses Destroys the Idol

Exodus 32

When God threatened to destroy his people, Moses answered, "No, Lord! Please don't do that. Remember your promise to make them a great nation and to give them the land of Canaan for their own? Please forgive the people and bless them as you promised."

God changed his mind about destroying his chosen people. Moses went down the mountain, carrying the stone tablets. As he got close to the camp, he heard the sound of a wild party, and when he saw what the people were doing, he was terribly angry with them. He threw the stone tablets down on the ground so hard that they broke.

Then he melted the calf-idol. When the gold had hardened, he ground it into powder. He put the powder into the water and made the people drink it.

Moses was angry with Aaron, too. Aaron tried to make excuses. He said, "The people insisted I give them a new god. I put the gold into the fire, and the idol just happened to come out." Of course that wasn't true. God punished the people for their sin of disobedience, and many of them died.

78
New Tablets and a New Agreement

Exodus 33–34

God was so disappointed in his people that he said he wouldn't go with them into the Promised Land. Moses begged the Lord to change his mind. He said, "If you don't go with us, how will all the people of the world know we are special to you?"

God replied, "All right. Because you ask it, I will go with you to Canaan. Now, prepare two more tablets of stone, just like the ones you broke."

Moses obeyed, and the next day he went alone to the mountain, taking the new tablets. God met him there and made a new covenant, or agreement, with him. God said he would do wonderful things for the people if they obeyed him faithfully. He told Moses not to make any peace treaties with their enemies in Canaan because God himself would destroy them.

God also told Moses more about how they should worship and about feasts they should have to celebrate the goodness of God. Moses promised to keep the agreement. Then God wrote the commandments again. Moses went down the mountain and joined his people. Because he had been with God, his face was shining.

79
Building God's House
Exodus 35–39

It was time to start to build the tabernacle. Moses invited all the people to bring gifts that could be used in the building and furnishing of the tabernacle. The people brought earrings, bracelets, and precious jewels. They gave valuable oil for lamps and beautiful cloth for the various hangings. Everything that went into the building and furnishing of the tabernacle was the very best and most beautiful that could be found or made. They wanted God's house of worship to be perfect.

A skilful workman named Bezalel made the ark of the covenant with its gold cover, called the mercy seat. This was the most important piece of furniture in the tabernacle because it was a symbol of God's presence with his people.

The workmen made the table, the altars, the lampstand and the lamps, and all the cloth hangings. Moses inspected everything to be sure it was all exactly like the pattern God had given him.

80
God's Glory Fills the Tabernacle

Exodus 40

Moses supervised the workers as they put the tabernacle together. They set up the ark, into which Moses had put the tablets with the Ten Commandments. They put a curtain around it, because this area was to be the Holy of Holies, a place where only the high priest could go. They put the other furniture where God had said it should go. Around the courtyard they hung the cloth curtains, to enclose the whole tabernacle area.

Ever since they had left Egypt, a great pillar of cloud had led them along. At night the cloud glowed red. Now this great cloud came and covered the tabernacle.

During the rest of their journey to Canaan, whenever the cloud moved, the people knew they should pack up the tabernacle and move with it. When the cloud stayed in the same place, the people stayed too.

When the tabernacle was finished, God's glory filled the place. It was so bright that Moses couldn't even go into the tabernacle.

— 81 —
The Wrong Kind of Fire

Leviticus 10

God told the people how they should worship him. Aaron and his four sons were to be leaders in this worship. God said that when the priests and the people followed his instructions, his glory would appear to them and he would accept their offerings. But if the people or the priests did not follow God's rules, God would not accept their sacrifices and would punish them.

The priests had to put some incense in special cups on top of fire they got from the altar. The people brought their sacrifices, and the priests offered them before the Lord. God sent his glory upon them, even sending fire from heaven to burn up the sacrifice. All the people shouted for joy and fell down on their faces before God.

But Nadab and Abihu, two of Aaron's sons, decided not to follow the rules. They put a different kind of fire in their incense cups. Immediately God punished them by sending fire from heaven to kill them. God told Aaron and his other two sons not to show any grief because Nadab and Abihu had been fairly punished for their sins.

— 82 —
Rules About Food

Leviticus 11

God was interested not only in his people's spiritual lives and their worship in the tabernacle. He also cared about their health, so he made special rules about what they should eat. The food they had permission to eat was called "clean", and the food they were forbidden to eat was called "unclean".

Animals: They should eat only those animals that chewed a cud and had divided hooves. Pigs were unclean because, although they have divided hooves, they don't chew a cud.

Fish: Fish that had both fins and scales were clean; those that had smooth skin or no fins were unclean.

Birds: Unclean birds were birds of prey, such as eagles, vultures, and hawks.

Insects: Insects that fly, crawl, or walk were declared unclean. Those that jump – like grasshoppers – were clean.

Small animals: Little animals that moved around on the ground were all called unclean – creatures like lizards, rats, and reptiles.

Not only were the Israelites not to eat all the unclean creatures, but they were not even to touch their dead bodies. God wanted to keep all disease and infection out of the Israelite camp.

— 83 —
Aaron's Special Work

Leviticus 16

God told Moses what Aaron, the high priest, should do in the tabernacle. He was the only person who was allowed to go into the inner room of the tabernacle, where the ark of the covenant was kept. This was called the Most Holy Place. Even Aaron could only go in once each year, on the Day of Atonement.

Before he could go into the Most Holy Place, he had to bathe himself and put on simple white clothing and make an animal sacrifice for his and his family's sins.

Aaron was to take a censer full of burning coals, some incense, and some of the blood of the bull he had sacrificed. He had to sprinkle some of the blood on the cover of the ark and in front of it.

Then he made a sacrifice for the sins of all the people of Israel and put some of that blood on the mercy seat also.

The blood offering had to be made, and only the high priest could do it.

While this was happening, the people of Israel were to stop their work and think about how sorry they were for their sins. If they were truly sorry, they would be forgiven.

84
Important Rules to Obey

Leviticus 17–22

God wanted his people to be like himself. Like him, they were to be fair, kind, loving, pure, and holy. God gave them instructions about getting along with other people and keeping their hearts and their actions pure.

He taught them to leave some of their grain and grapes in the fields for poor people. He said they should never steal nor tell lies. If they owed other people money, they should pay it as soon as possible. They should be loving and kind, to each other and to foreigners who might live nearby. They must never take advantage of disabled people.

God said, "You must never copy what your ungodly neighbours do, worshipping false gods by sacrificing their children and having the wrong kinds of sexual relationships with others." He made it very clear that his people were to be different from other people in the world because they were his chosen ones – chosen to show God's character and his glory. So he set very high standards for them and expected them to obey him perfectly.

85
Special Holidays

Leviticus 23–24

God told the people of Israel to observe special holidays. One of these was the Sabbath, the day on which they rested and worshipped God, remembering how

God rested after creating the world and everything in it.

Three of their most important holidays were:

1. The Passover. This reminded them of how God passed over the homes of his people when he killed the firstborn children of the Egyptians and helped his people escape from Egypt.

2. The Harvest Festival. This was a day of thanksgiving after all the crops had been gathered. The people were to praise God for sending the rain and sunshine.

3. The Tabernacle Festival. This reminded the people of the way they lived as they travelled from Egypt to Canaan, the Promised Land. For a whole week they were to move out of their regular houses and live in huts formed from tree branches woven together. At each of these celebrations, the people were to bring gifts to God – olive oil for the lamps in the tabernacle and fresh bread to put on the gold table.

86

A Big Celebration

Leviticus 25

Every seven years the people of Israel had a Sabbath year, when they rested and didn't plant any crops. After seven of those Sabbath years, God gave them a year of special celebration on the fiftieth year. It was called the Year of Jubilee.

During that year the people didn't grow crops but had plenty to eat because they had saved food from the year before. Also, if they had had to sell any of their land to pay their debts, on the Year of Jubilee they would get their land back, reminding them that the land really belonged to God and was theirs only as his gift.

The Israelites were told to be especially kind to each other and to foreigners among them during that year. God said, "If any of your fellow Israelites have become your slaves because they owed you money, you must let them go free." All the people were very glad when it was time for a Year of Jubilee because so many good things happened to them during that year!

87

The Levites Work in the Tabernacle

Numbers 1–4

More than a year after they had left Egypt, the people of Israel moved on from Mount Sinai. Moses and Aaron counted over six thousand men who could be soldiers. They came from every tribe except the Levites. The Levites

had the special job of looking after the tabernacle and were not to fight in wars.

When it was time to move, the Levites had to take the tabernacle apart and carry it as they were travelling. Most of the tabernacle was carried in wagons, but the ark, the lampstand, and the gold and bronze altars had to be carried on the shoulders of Levites. When the cloud stopped and the people stopped to make camp, the Levites put the tabernacle together again.

The Levites were also the ones who made all the sacrifices when the people brought animals as their offerings to God. They carried wood to burn and water for washing, and then they had to carry the ashes away from the altars after the sacrifices were burned.

It was a great privilege to be a Levite and work in the tabernacle.

88

Too Much Meat!

Numbers 11

The people left Mount Sinai. When the cloud stopped, they camped. They started complaining to Moses. "We haven't had a decent meal since we left Egypt. Now all we have is this manna, and we're getting tired of it!"

The Lord heard them grumbling, and he was angry with them. He had rescued them and led them safely away from their cruel masters. Moses was discouraged too. He said, "Lord, why did you make me leader of such ungrateful people? If they are going to behave like this, I'd rather die right now!"

God said that he would appoint seventy helpers for Moses. Then God told Moses that he would send meat to the people for a month.

"They will have all they can eat. They will grow to hate the sight of it! That will teach them not to complain all the time."

He sent a great flock of quail that flew into the camp. The people had plenty of meat, but some of them got sick and died as a punishment for their complaining.

89
Miriam and Aaron Criticize Moses

Numbers 12

Moses' brother and sister began to criticize him. Miriam and Aaron were jealous of Moses' position of leadership, and they talked against him. "Is Moses the only one who can speak for God? Why couldn't he speak through us, too?" They also criticized him because he had married a woman who wasn't an Israelite.

God called Moses, Aaron, and Miriam to the door of the tabernacle. He said to Aaron and Miriam, "I chose Moses for this task. You should be afraid to criticize him. I speak directly to him, face-to-face."

Then God left, very angry with Aaron and Miriam. Miriam's skin suddenly became white with the disease of leprosy. When Aaron saw that, he told Moses he was sorry about criticizing him, and he begged Moses not to let Miriam have leprosy. Moses didn't want his sister to have leprosy either and begged God to heal her.

God said that she must stay outside the camp for seven days, and then she

would be healed and could return. She and Aaron had learned a lesson the hard way.

90
Checking Out the Land

Numbers 13

The people of Israel were near the border of Canaan, the Promised Land. God said to Moses, "Send one man from each of the twelve tribes into Canaan to check out the people and see whether the cities are strongly protected. Also find out whether the land is good for farming and whether there are lots of trees. Tell the spies to bring back some samples of the fruit of the land."

The twelve spies explored Canaan and brought back grapes, pomegranates, and figs, showing what good land it was.

When the spies returned, most of them said, "It is a fertile and beautiful land. But the people who live there are very large and fierce. We really can't win if we try to drive them out of the land."

But two of the spies didn't agree. Caleb and Joshua said, "God has promised to give us this land, so we don't need to be afraid. It's a wonderful country, and we should march right in and start to live there. We can trust God!"

91
Punishment for Disobedience

Numbers 14

Well, when the Israelites heard both sides of the spies' report, they chose to believe the ten who thought they

would be wiped out if they fought with the fierce tribes in Canaan. Once more they started to complain about Moses' and Aaron's leadership. They shouted to each other, "If only we had stayed in Egypt or had died in the wilderness! We were better off in Egypt. Let's choose a new leader who will take us back."

Again Caleb and Joshua tried to remind them of God's promise of victory, but the people wouldn't listen. Then, suddenly, the glory of God appeared in the camp, and God spoke to Moses: "That's it! I've heard enough. How long will these people rebel against me? I'm going to wipe them out with a plague. Moses, I'll make you a great nation instead of them."

Moses said, "Oh, no, Lord! If you do that, everyone will think you couldn't take care of your people. Please forgive our sins and let us continue to be the great nation you promised."

God decided to listen to Moses and give the people another chance. However, their punishment was that instead of getting to go right into Canaan, they had to go back into the wilderness and wander around for 40 years – a year for each of the 40 days the spies had explored Canaan. The ten unfaithful spies were struck dead, but Caleb and Joshua were rewarded for their faith.

92
The Earth Swallows Korah

Numbers 16

As if the people hadn't complained enough about Moses, Korah and three of his friends stirred up more trouble by persuading 250 important leaders to join them in a rebellion against Moses and Aaron. They said to Moses, "We are tired of your ordering us around. You are no better than the rest of us. Why should Aaron get to be high priest?"

Moses prayed; then he answered them, "We'll find out whether God has really chosen us. Come back tomorrow with fire in your incense burners, and we'll see what God has to say."

The next day they were back with their censers. The people of Israel gathered around Korah and the other rebels. Then Moses spoke to Korah: "Aren't you satisfied to be a worker in God's house of worship? Must you try to take the place of God's appointed servant?"

Then Moses warned everyone to get away from Korah and the rebels. He said, "God will show you who should be your leaders." As soon as he had finished speaking, the earth opened and swallowed up Korah and his rebellious friends.

93
Buds, Blossoms, and Fruit

Numbers 16–17

The people of Israel were afraid when Korah and the rebels were punished by God. They ran away so they wouldn't be killed too. As they thought about what had happened to Korah, they became angry and started criticizing Moses and Aaron again. While they were grumbling, they suddenly saw the cloud over the tabernacle. This showed that God was present.

Then God spoke, saying, "I'm going

to destroy these stubborn people."

Moses and Aaron prayed for them, but almost fifteen thousand people died.

God said, "Now I'll stop all this grumbling against my chosen leaders. Moses, tell the chief of each tribe to carve his name on a wooden rod. The rod from the tribe of Levi should have Aaron's name on it. Put the rods in front of the ark in the tabernacle. The true leader's rod will sprout buds."

Moses followed God's instructions. The next day Aaron's rod had not only buds on it but blossoms and ripe almonds too! From that time on, Aaron's rod was always kept in the tabernacle. Whenever anyone complained, Moses showed him the rod.

94

Moses Loses His Temper

Numbers 20

The people moved on to the Zin Desert, where Moses' sister, Miriam, died. When they ran out of water, they blamed Moses! "Why didn't you just kill us along with Korah?"

God told Moses and Aaron to take Aaron's rod and stand in front of a certain rock. "Speak to that rock, and water will gush out."

Moses went to the rock, but then he lost his temper. He shouted, "You stubborn rebels! Must I always get water for you?" Then he hit the rock twice with the rod. Immediately water gushed out, and everyone had plenty to drink.

But God said, "You didn't obey me. Because you struck the rock instead of speaking to it, you and Aaron may not

enter the Promised Land."

Soon the Lord told Moses it was time for Aaron to die. He said, "Take Aaron and his son Eleazar up onto Mount Hor." Then God told Moses to remove Aaron's priestly clothing and put it on Eleazar. As Moses did this, Aaron died. Moses and Eleazar descended from the mountain to join the people who were waiting at the bottom.

"God has appointed Eleazar to take Aaron's place," Moses told the people.

95

Bitten by Poisonous Snakes

Numbers 21

The people had been travelling for almost forty years, and everyone was getting tired and discouraged. Once again they grumbled at Moses. "We don't have enough water and food, and we are tired of eating manna."

Their ungrateful attitude angered God, so he punished them by sending poisonous snakes into the camp to bite them. Many died. The people were sorry that they had complained, so they cried to Moses, "Please pray that God will take the snakes away and save our lives."

Moses asked the Lord to help his people. God said, "Make a snake out of bronze, and fasten it to the top of a long pole. Raise it high over the camp where people can look up at it. Everyone who does so will be healed of snakebite and will not die." Moses did this, and many lives were spared.

Moses needed permission for the Israelites to travel through some land belonging to King Sihon, a powerful

Amorite king. King Sihon refused and attacked the Israelites at Jahaz. But the Israelites won and were able to travel throughout the land of the Amorites.

96

The Talking Donkey

Numbers 22

When the Israelites came near the plains of Moab, King Balak became frightened. He had heard what they had done to the armies of the Amorites! He sent messengers to offer money to Balaam if he would curse Israel.

Balaam wanted the money, so he saddled his donkey and followed the king's messengers. But God didn't want anyone to curse his special people, so he sent an angel to stop Balaam. The angel stood in front of Balaam with a sword in his hand. Balaam couldn't see the angel, but his donkey could. The donkey turned away and left the road. Balaam didn't understand, so he beat the donkey.

Further along the road, the donkey saw the angel again. There was a wall on either side, and, frightened, she pressed up against it, crushing Balaam's foot. This made him angry, so he beat her again.

On the third occasion, the donkey collapsed under Balaam. Again he beat her. This time an amazing thing happened: the donkey spoke, asking, "Why have you beaten me three times?"

Then the Lord let Balaam see the angel, and Balaam was sorry he had treated the donkey so badly. The angel told him to go and see King Balak but say only what God told him.

97

Curses Turn to Blessings

Numbers 23–25

Balaam went on with Balak's messengers, and the king came out to meet him. "At last you are here," he said. "Yes," said Balaam, "but I'll speak only what God puts in my mouth." The next day Balaam told Balak to build seven altars and prepare seven bulls and seven rams for sacrifice. He and King Balak each sacrificed a bull and a ram. Then Balaam asked God what to say about Israel. God told him, and when Balaam spoke, everything he said was a blessing upon the people of Israel.

This made Balak really angry. He took Balaam to a different place, and they built seven more altars and made sacrifices. Again Balaam asked God's advice, and again he was allowed to speak only good things.

Balak said, "Maybe you can't curse my enemies, but don't bless them!" The same thing happened again, and so Balak said, "Go home, but don't expect any pay."

Balak thought of another way to bring trouble upon Israel. He threw a party to honour Canaanite idols. He invited some young Israelites, and soon they started to worship the false gods along with the Canaanites. As Balak had expected, God became angry, and he sent a disease that killed thousands of his people.

98

The View Across the River

Numbers 25–26

The forty years of wandering were almost over. Before God could let the people go into the Promised Land, he had to be sure all of the older generation had died, so he asked Moses to count the people. Caleb and Joshua had been faithful, trusting spies and were the only older people allowed to go into Canaan. Because the people of Midian had led many of the Israelites into idol worship, God said his people must make war on Midian. So they killed all the Midianites and kept their animals and burned down all their cities.

After the war, God's people were grateful because not one of the Israelite soldiers had been killed. To show their gratitude, they offered to Moses and Eleazar all the jewellery they had taken from the Midianites. Moses and Eleazar accepted the jewellery and put it in the tabernacle as a thank-offering to God.

At last the people of Israel stood on the banks of the Jordan River. They looked across it into the Promised Land and thanked the Lord that it was almost time to enter Canaan.

99
The People Are Divided

Numbers 32

The tribes of Reuben, Gad, and the half-tribe of Manasseh were camped beside the Jordan River. They asked Moses if they could make their permanent home there instead of on the opposite side of the river, where the other tribes would be settling.

Moses got angry with them. "What's the matter? Are you so afraid of the people in Canaan that you want to avoid a war with them? Do you want the other tribes to do your fighting for you?"

"No, not at all," they replied. "But the land on this side of the river looks like a wonderful place for our flocks and herds, because there's plenty of pastureland. We want to leave our families and animals here and come across the river with everyone else. We'll fight until the Canaanites are destroyed. Then we can come back here and settle down with our families."

Moses thought it over. He asked everyone else who was camped by the river what they thought. Everyone agreed to let them have the land they wanted, if they helped to wipe out the Canaanite enemies first.

100
Safe from Revenge

Numbers 35

Moses made plans for when his people would be living in Canaan, the Promised Land, without him because of his earlier disobedience. He told them that certain cities were to be given to the Levites for their special use. Each of those cities would have plenty of pastureland around it for their flocks.

Other special cities were to be called cities of refuge, or cities of safety. Those cities were places where someone could run for safety if he had accidentally killed someone. A relative of the dead person might try to get revenge on the killer. But once a killer was inside a city of safety and had told his story to the judges there, no one could harm him. The killer had to stay in the city of safety until after the death of the high priest. Then he could go back home, and no one could punish him for the accidental killing. The cities of safety were not intended to protect murderers but only those who had not meant to cause another person's death.

101
Moses' Long Speech

Deuteronomy 32–34

Since Moses wasn't going into Canaan, he made a long speech, reminding his people of everything that had happened since they left Egypt. He didn't want them to forget God's goodness during the past forty years.

Moses had seen how easily the people forgot God's instructions and how often they disobeyed God. He reminded them of all the commandments that told them how God wanted them to live. He said, "Don't forget: You must never worship any other God. Don't make idols or worship them. Don't use God's name carelessly, and always keep the Sabbath day holy. Honour your father and mother. You must never murder or commit adultery or steal or lie. And you must not desire anything that belongs to someone else." Then he reminded them about the other 613 rules. And he repeated what they had learned about the feasts and festivals they were to observe, each one a reminder of the good things God had done for them.

Finally he told them that Joshua was to be their new leader.

Then he climbed to the top of Mount Nebo and looked across the river at the Promised Land. And there Moses died at the age of 120.

102
Joshua Becomes the Leader

Joshua 1

After Moses died, Joshua became the leader of the people of Israel. He had been Moses' assistant and one of the two faithful spies who had brought back a good report from Canaan and had encouraged the people to trust God for safety.

God said to Joshua, "Get the people ready to cross the Jordan River. I will give you all the land you walk on. Don't be afraid to go into Canaan. I will be with you and will take care of you. Just obey me and be brave."

Joshua told the people to get ready

to cross the river. He reminded the tribes of Reuben, Gad, and the half-tribe of Manasseh that their wives and children could stay on the east side of the river, but they must go across and help the other tribes get rid of the hostile Canaanites, as God had directed them. Later, when the wars were over, they could rejoin their families and go on being herdsmen on their fertile plots of land. Everyone promised to obey and follow Joshua because God had chosen him to be the leader.

— 103 —
Rahab Helps the Spies

Joshua 2

Joshua sent in two more spies for a last look around before he took the thousands of Israelites into Canaan. The two spies quietly crossed the river and went to an inn owned by Rahab. The king heard a rumour that spies had come to Jericho, so he sent some men to capture them.

Rahab, warned that the king's men were coming, hid the two spies under some piles of grain that were drying on the roof. When the king's men came, she told them the spies had already left. "Hurry," she said, "you might be able to catch them before they leave the city."

Then she went to the spies and said, "I know how successful you have been. You must worship a very powerful God. I know that your God will give you the victory over Jericho. I want you to save me and my family because we have helped you today." The spies told Rahab to hang a red rope in the window of her

home and stay inside with her family. When the people of Israel captured the city, they would see the rope and know that it was Rahab's home.

104
Crossing the River

Joshua 3–4

The spies returned to the camp, and the people gathered by the Jordan River, ready to cross. The next morning the priests appointed to carry the ark went first. As they stepped into the water, the river stopped flowing, and the priests walked into the middle of it. While they held up the ark, everyone else crossed safely over.

God told Joshua, "Choose twelve men, one from each tribe, to pick up twelve large stones from the middle of the riverbed and carry them to the far bank. The priests should stay in the middle of the riverbed."

When everyone was safely on the other side, the priests continued to cross the riverbed. As soon as they stepped onto the bank, the water started to flow again!

The people made a camp at a place called Gilgal. They used the twelve stones from the riverbed to build a monument. Joshua said, "One day your children and grandchildren will ask, 'What is that stone monument for?' You must tell them about this wonderful day when God opened up the waters of the Jordan River and let his people walk across on dry land. He did this to show everyone how powerful he is."

105
The Lord Visits Joshua

Joshua 5

The people of Israel were happy to be in Canaan. One of the first things they did was to celebrate the Passover, reminding them of the night when the Angel of the Lord passed over their homes.

In Gilgal they were glad to find some corn growing in the fields because they were tired of eating manna. Now that they were in a country where they could find food and could start growing crops, the manna soon stopped appearing on the ground.

Joshua knew that one of his biggest jobs would be to capture Jericho and occupy it. As he was thinking about how he and his army could successfully make war on Jericho, a man appeared to him, holding a sword in his hand. Joshua asked, "Are you for us or for our enemies?"

The man replied, "I have come as the commander in chief of the Lord's army."

Joshua knew that the man was really the Lord himself, so he fell down and worshipped him.

Then the commander said to him, as he had said to Moses at the burning bush, "Take off your shoes. You are standing on holy ground."

106
A City's Walls Fall Down

Joshua 6

The commander of the Lord's army told Joshua that God would give him the victory. He told him exactly how to win the battle. Joshua agreed to obey what the Lord told him to do.

Joshua's soldiers marched around the city wall with the priests who carried the ark of the covenant. Ahead of the ark walked seven priests blowing trumpets. The army and the priests did this every day for six days.

On the seventh day everyone started marching earlier than usual because this time they had to march around the walls of Jericho seven times. As usual, the seven priests blew on their trumpets while they were marching. At the end of the seventh time, the priests gave a loud blast and Joshua ordered, "Shout aloud, for the Lord has given you victory over the city!" The soldiers shouted, and the walls fell down with a great crash!

The soldiers marched into Jericho

and captured it, but they remembered to take care of Rahab and her family. Then the army burned the city down, but they put the valuable things into the Lord's treasury.

107
Why Did Ai Defeat Israel?

Joshua 7

Joshua wanted to conquer Ai. He asked some scouts to find out how well fortified it was. When they returned they said, "There are only a few soldiers protecting it, so we will need only two or three thousand men."

Joshua sent three thousand men, but the soldiers at Ai defeated them easily and killed thirty-six men. Others died while the Israelite troops were in retreat. Joshua's army was terrified by this defeat. Joshua fell on his face and asked God, "Did you bring us into Canaan to let us be defeated by our enemies? Now the Canaanite tribes will no longer respect our God. They will attack us and wipe us out."

God replied, "Get up! This has happened because someone has disobeyed me and taken some of the valuables from Jericho instead of destroying everything as I commanded. Tell everyone to appear before me, and I will point out the guilty one."

The people came before the Lord, and he showed that Achan, from the tribe of Judah, was guilty. Achan confessed, "I stole some silver, gold, and a beautiful robe and hid them in my tent."

108
Punishment for a Thief

Joshua 7–8

Joshua had Achan's tent searched. The stolen goods were found buried under the tent. The men took them to Joshua. Joshua said to Achan, "What you have done has brought trouble to all of us. Now the Lord will bring disaster to you."

The men of Israel stoned Achan and his family to death. Their bodies were burned and then buried under a big pile of stones. That place became known as the Valley of Trouble.

The Lord said to Joshua, "Now you will be able to defeat the army at Ai. You must destroy everyone living there, but this time your people may keep the gold and silver instead of putting it into my treasury." So Joshua and his army attacked Ai again. This time Joshua took his whole army. He sent thirty thousand of his soldiers behind the city while the rest attacked from the front. When the soldiers of Ai came out to fight their attackers, the thirty thousand men set the city on fire.

The men of Ai were trapped between the burning city and the Israelite army. Joshua's army completely destroyed them.

109
A Bad Peace Treaty

Joshua 9

When the kings of the Canaanite tribes saw what the Israelites had done to Jericho and Ai, they were afraid. They joined together and planned to attack them. But the Gibeonites tried another way to protect themselves.

They sent a group to see Joshua. They loaded their donkeys with old sacks and brittle wineskins, and they carried mouldy bread with them. They wore patched-up sandals and ragged clothes so Joshua would think they had been travelling for a long time. When they came to the Israelite camp, they said to Joshua, "We want you to make a treaty with us."

Joshua told the Gibeonites, "I can't make a treaty with you because you may be one of my neighbouring tribes. God has said I must destroy all the heathen Canaanite nations because he has given this land to us."

The Gibeonites answered, "We're from far away. Our clothes and sandals were new when we left. Look at them now. And this bread was fresh." Joshua should have asked the Lord's advice, but he didn't. He believed the Gibeonites and signed the treaty.

110
The Sun Stands Still

Joshua 10

A few days later Joshua found out that the Gibeonites were a neighbouring Canaanite tribe. He asked them, "Why did you trick me?" The Gibeonites said, "We heard about the victories you were winning, and we were afraid. We wanted to stop you from attacking us." The people of Israel wanted to kill them, but Joshua said, "No, we must honour our treaty." And so he made them slaves.

When the king of Jerusalem heard about the treaty, he was worried because Gibeon was a large, powerful city. He asked four other kings to help him make war on Gibeon. When they began

their siege, the Gibeonites sent for Joshua. "Please come and help us fight our enemies."

Joshua took his army and went to help Gibeon. The Lord promised to help him defeat the combined army of the five nations. He did this by sending big hailstones that killed more soldiers than the Israelite army did! Then Joshua prayed, "Let the sun stand still over Gibeon and the moon over the Valley of Aijalon."

God answered Joshua's prayer, and for almost a whole day and night, the sun and moon stood still, and Joshua was able to finish defeating the five kings and their armies.

111
A Special Place for Levites

Joshua 18–21

During their travels in the wilderness, the people of Israel had been carrying the tabernacle around with them. Now that they had entered the Promised Land and had chosen to settle in the city of Shiloh, the priests and Levites could set up the tabernacle for the last time.

The tribes of Israel were getting tired of fighting to clear out the Canaanite tribes from the Promised Land. Joshua called the people together and reminded them that there was still land to be conquered and occupied. He sent out some scouts and asked them for a written report and some maps showing where their enemies were.

Then Joshua drew straws to find out what part of the land should go to each tribe. He told them, "God says you must finish driving out the heathen tribes, and he will help you gain the victory over them."

God told the priests and Levites they would not have farmland like the other tribes because their work was in the tabernacle. But they would have special cities where they could live with their wives and children.

112
The People Choose God

Joshua 22–24

It was time for the people of Reuben, Gad, and Manasseh to go back to their land on the east side of the Jordan River. Joshua thanked them for helping the other tribes fight for their land. He said to them, "Be sure to love the Lord and serve him faithfully."

They built an altar like the one at the tabernacle in Shiloh. The other tribes were upset because God had said there must be only one place of sacrifice. They sent the high priest to scold them. But the eastern tribes said, "This is only a monument to express our gratitude to God and to remind us that we are still Israelites even though we are on the opposite side of the river." So everyone understood and was happy.

Joshua called all the people together and reminded them of God's wonderful care. "He has given you this beautiful place to live and has driven out your enemies. Be sure that you never forget to love him and worship him as you should. My family and I are always going to serve the Lord."

And all the people replied, "We will serve him forever. We will never worship false gods or idols." Joshua set up a big rock near the tabernacle to remind them of that promise.

113
Israel Needs New Leaders

Joshua 24 – Judges 2

Joshua died, and the people buried him on a hillside. The Israelites had served the Lord throughout Joshua's lifetime, and they kept on being faithful to God as long as the elders of Israel were alive.

Some of the Israelite tribes went on fighting the Canaanites for the territories God had promised them. But gradually they became careless about obeying God's instructions. They didn't destroy all the cities, and they didn't break down all the idols and heathen altars.

In some parts of Canaan, the Israelites made friends with some of the wicked tribes. Some of them even married people from the enemy nations. This led the Israelites to worship the heathen gods of the Canaanites. When God saw what was happening, he sent troops to defeat the people of Israel and make them slaves. The Israelites said they were sorry and would try to follow the Lord again.

Each time this happened, God would forgive them and give them a strong leader to help them do the right thing. These leaders were called "judges". The book of Judges tells us about twelve judges who tried to guide Israel in following the Lord.

114
The First Judges

Judges 2–3

When the people of Israel turned away from God and started to worship the Canaanite gods, Baal and the Ashtoreths, God was angry. He stopped protecting them, and soon they became slaves of the king of Mesopotamia. For eight years they served this king, but finally they remembered their true God and prayed that he would help them.

God chose a strong leader to rescue them. The leader, or judge, was Othniel. God sent his Spirit to Othniel, and Othniel saved the Israelites from the king of Mesopotamia. For forty years they obeyed God and had peace in the land.

When Othniel died, the people began to forget God again. They became subjects of a Moabite king named Eglon, and they had to pay heavy taxes to him. Then God sent Ehud, a Benjamite, to help them. Ehud went to see King Eglon and pretended he needed to talk to him alone. The king's aides left, and then Ehud stabbed Eglon. By the time the king's men found Eglon, Ehud had escaped. He led Israel in war against the Moabites. Israel won, and for eighty years they had peace.

The next judge was Shamgar, and he helped the Israelites get victory over the Philistines. But soon the people forgot God again.

115
Deborah Leads an Army

Judges 4

For about twenty years the Israelites had to serve King Jabin. The head of his army was a cruel man named Sisera. The people of Israel used to come to Deborah, a prophetess, and she would settle their problems with wise decisions.

Deborah sent for Barak and said, "God wants you to lead the fight against General Sisera. God will give you the victory."

But Barak was afraid. "I can't go to war unless you go with me."

Deborah said, "All right, but a woman will get the credit, not you."

They gathered an army of ten thousand men and marched into battle.

God sent confusion and panic into the enemy forces, and Barak's troops destroyed every one of them – except Sisera, who fled. He escaped to the camp of some allies of King Jabin. A woman named Jael invited him to hide in her tent. She gave him a drink of milk and told him to rest. When Sisera was asleep, Jael killed him by hammering a sharp tent peg through his head.

When Barak came by, chasing Sisera, Jael showed him Sisera's body. Soon afterward Jabin and his people were completely destroyed.

— 116 —
God Chooses Gideon as Leader

Judges 6

After forty peaceful years, Israel again started to worship other gods. The Lord sent the

Midianites against them, and for seven years the people suffered terribly. They cried to God for help, and he chose a leader named Gideon. Gideon was threshing grain secretly in a grape press when the Angel of the Lord appeared and said, "The Lord is with you, mighty warrior!"

Gideon replied bitterly, "If the Lord is with us, why has he left us to the mercy of Midian? Besides, I'm not a mighty warrior. I'm just a farm boy."

"God will use you to get your people out of trouble," the Lord answered.

"How can I be sure? Wait here, and I'll bring you an offering." Gideon got meat, broth, and bread.

The Lord told him to put the bread and meat on a rock and pour the broth over it. The Lord touched it with his walking stick, and fire flamed up from the rock, burning up the offering. Immediately the Lord disappeared. Gideon was afraid he would die because he had seen the Lord, but the voice of the Lord said, "Don't worry. You won't die." Gideon built an altar there and called it "Peace with God".

117

Is the Wool Wet or Dry?

Judges 6

That night the Lord told Gideon to tear down his father's altar to Baal and break down the idols. "Then build an altar to the Lord and sacrifice a young bull. Use one of the idols as wood for the fire." Gideon was afraid, but he obeyed.

In the morning the village men were amazed at what they saw. When they found out Gideon had done it, they said, "He must die because of what he did to Baal's altar and the idols."

But Gideon's father said, "Why are you defending Baal? If he's a real god, he can take care of himself." So the men left Gideon alone.

God sent his Spirit to Gideon, and Gideon gathered an army to fight the Midianites. He asked the Lord for a sign to prove that he would help. "I'll put some wool on the barn floor. In the morning, if the wool is wet and the floor dry, I'll know you are with me."

In the morning, the floor was dry but the wool was soaking wet. Gideon asked the Lord for one more sign. This time he wanted the floor to be wet and the wool dry. And the Lord did just as Gideon asked.

118
Gideon's Army Wins

Judges 7

Gideon gathered about thirty-two thousand men to fight the Midianites. The Lord said, "Send home all who are fearful about the battle." About twenty-two thousand of them went home. Then God said, "You still have too many. Take them down to the edge of the water, and let them drink water from the spring. Those who pick up water in their hands and lap it like dogs are the ones you should take into battle. Send home those who get down on their knees and drink from the spring."

Only three hundred soldiers drank from their hands. The Lord said, "I'll conquer the Midianites with these men."

Gideon gave each soldier a trumpet and a pitcher containing a lighted lamp. He said, "When we get close to the Midianites' camp, we will blow our trumpets, break our pitchers, and shout, 'The sword of the Lord and

of Gideon!'" When they broke their pitchers and shouted, the Midianites were frightened. The noise and lights made them think there were more soldiers than there were.

Gideon's army defeated them and captured their two kings. At last Israel was free of the cruel Midianites.

119
Jephthah's Foolish Promise

Judges 11

Jephthah was a brave Israelite soldier. He decided to move to another country after a family quarrel. Sometime later, the Ammonites attacked Israel, trying to get back the land the Israelites had taken from them. Israel needed a strong leader. They sent for Jephthah, but he didn't want to come because they only wanted him when they were in trouble.

They promised that if he would win the war, they would make him king. So he agreed to come.

Jephthah made a vow that if God would help him win the victory, he would offer him the first thing that came out of his house when he got home. Jephthah won the war, but when he got home the first thing that came out of his house was his own little daughter! God would have excused him from his vow, since it was against the Law to sacrifice one's child, but Jephthah kept his word. For many years, the young women of Israel had a time of mourning for Jephthah's daughter.

120
A Miracle Baby

Judges 13

After a while the Israelites sinned against God again, so God allowed the Philistines to rule over them for forty years. Manoah and his wife were childless, but one day the Angel of the Lord came to Manoah's wife and said, "You are going to have a baby. When the baby comes, he is to be a Nazirite, a special servant of mine. He must not drink wine or cut his hair or beard. He will free Israel from the Philistines."

Manoah's wife told Manoah what had happened. Manoah wanted to see the Angel. The Angel returned, and Manoah talked to him. Neither Manoah nor his wife realized who their visitor was. When they asked him his name, he said it was a secret.

Manoah prepared some meat and grain for a sacrifice. When he put it on the altar, a fire sprang up and burned the sacrifice. Then the Angel of the Lord went up to heaven in the flames! Manoah realized they had seen the Lord, and he was afraid. But his wife said, "Don't worry. He didn't come to hurt us."

She had the baby. They named him Samson and dedicated him to God's service.

121
Samson Kills a Lion

Judges 14

Samson's parents wanted him to marry an Israelite girl, but he insisted on marrying a Philistine woman. On the way to her home, a lion attacked Samson and his parents. God's Spirit gave Samson strength to kill the lion with his bare hands.

Sometime later Samson saw that bees had made a hive in the lion's carcass and that the carcass was full of honey.

Samson gave a wedding feast. He challenged thirty young men to a contest. "If you guess the answer to a riddle," he said, "I'll give you each some new clothes. If you cannot answer, you must each give me some clothes."

"What's the riddle?" they asked.

"Food came out of the eater and sweetness came out of the strong," Samson said.

Samson's bride cried until he told her the answer. At the end of the contest the young Philistine men answered, "What is sweeter than honey, and what is stronger than a lion?"

Samson realized that his bride had told them the answer. Her disloyalty made him angry, so Samson deserted his new wife and went back to Israel.

122

Samson Punishes His Enemies

Judges 15

After a while, Samson calmed down, so he went to see his wife. Her father said, "I thought you weren't coming back, so I let your best man marry her." Samson was furious. He caught three hundred foxes, tied their tails together, and fastened a burning torch to each pair. The foxes ran through the Philistines' fields, setting fire to all their crops.

When the Philistines found out why he had done this, they killed the girl and her father. That made Samson even angrier. He attacked and killed more Philistines. For a time he stayed in Judah. The Philistines chased Samson and asked the men of Judah to help them capture him. The men of Judah told Samson to stop upsetting the Philistines and wanted to turn him over to the Philistines themselves. Samson said, "Just don't kill me yourselves."

The men of Judah tied him up with some new ropes and took him to the

Philistines. Then the Spirit of God made Samson very strong. He broke the ropes, grabbed the jawbone of a dead donkey, and used it to kill a thousand Philistines.

— 123 —
An Unfaithful Girlfriend

Judges 16

Samson had a girlfriend named Delilah. The Philistines promised her a lot of money if she would find out what made Samson so strong and help them capture him. She begged Samson to tell her the secret of his strength. He told her he would be weak if he was tied up with leather bowstrings. She tied him up, and then said, "The Philistines are coming!" But he snapped the leather thongs easily.

Delilah tried again. Samson said he could be tied with new ropes. But again he broke the ropes with no trouble. Next he said, "If you weave my hair into a loom, I can't get away." But again he got loose very easily.

Delilah nagged Samson until he told her his secret. "If my hair is cut, I will be no stronger than other men." Delilah knew he was telling the truth, so she sent for the Philistines. They brought the money and hid nearby. While Samson was asleep, a man came and cut off his hair. Then Delilah called, "Samson! The Philistines are coming!" This time Samson couldn't escape.

— 124 —
Samson's Enemies Capture Him

Judges 16

The Philistines took Samson to a prison in Gaza. They blinded him and chained him up. Samson had to grind the grain for the prison. But Samson's hair began to grow again!

The Philistines decided to have a

big celebration and make sacrifices to their god, Dagon, because they thought Dagon had helped them capture Samson. The people got drunk and had Samson brought before them, led by a young boy. Samson stood in the centre of the temple, which was crowded with thousands of jeering Philistines. "Put one of my hands on each large pillar," he told the boy. Then Samson prayed, "O God, please give me back my strength just one more time, so I can punish the Philistines for taking away my sight."

Samson started to push very hard on the two pillars. He cried out, "Let me die with the Philistines!" And the temple collapsed, crushing all the people, including Samson himself. In his death Samson killed more Philistines than he had during his whole life.

— 125 —
Naomi and Ruth

Ruth 1

There was a famine in Judah, so a man called Elimelech took his wife, Naomi, and his two sons to Moab to find food. After a while Elimelech died. When his sons grew up, they married Moabite girls named Orpah and Ruth. But both the sons died too, leaving Naomi without any men to care for her.

When she heard that the famine was over, she decided to return to Judah. She tried to send her daughters-in-law back to their parents. Orpah agreed to go, but Ruth insisted on going with her mother-in-law. Ruth said, "I want to stay with you and your people. And I want to worship your God."

So Naomi agreed, and they walked to her hometown, Bethlehem. The village women saw her and asked, "Isn't that Naomi?"

"Don't call me that," Naomi said. "That name means 'pleasant'. My name should be 'Mara', which means 'bitter', because my life has been really bitter. I went to Moab with a husband and sons, but I have come back without them. God has turned his back on me."

— 126 —
Ruth Works in the Fields

Ruth 2

Naomi and Ruth had arrived in Bethlehem at the beginning of the barley harvest. They needed food, so Ruth went to the fields to pick up the grain that the reapers dropped. The Law said that dropped grain had to be left for the poor. Ruth worked in the fields of a farmer named Boaz.

Boaz saw Ruth in the field, and when he learned that she was Naomi's daughter-in-law, Boaz wanted to help her because he had heard how kind she had been to Naomi. Boaz told Ruth she was welcome to come every day and take all the grain she wanted.

Boaz told his farm workers to "drop" extra grain for Ruth and to treat her respectfully. At the end of the day Ruth had gathered about a half-bushel of grain to take home. Naomi was amazed

when she saw it. "What farmer has been so kind to you?" she asked. When Naomi learned it was Boaz, she realized he was a rich relative of Elimelech's. She told Ruth to keep going to his field to gather grain every day.

127
Ruth and Boaz Are Married

Ruth 3–4

Ruth worked in Boaz's field all through harvest time. One day Naomi explained who Boaz was. Naomi told Ruth to go to his threshing floor that night and to lie quietly by his feet.

Ruth did as Naomi had said. When Boaz woke up and saw Ruth, he was surprised. "What do you want?" he asked.

"Please cover me with your garment because you are my close relative," said Ruth. She was asking him to show that he would accept his responsibility, as her nearest relative, to marry and protect her. That was the custom in those days.

Boaz said, "I would like to marry you, but I know a man who is even more closely related to you than I am. I'll ask him if he wants to marry you. If he doesn't, I will gladly become your husband."

The other man said he could not marry Ruth, so Boaz took her as his wife. They had a baby boy and named him Obed. Naomi was a happy grandmother, helping to take care of the baby.

When Obed grew up, he became the father of Jesse and the grandfather of King David.

128
Job's Troubles

Job 1–2

Job was a very rich man who lived in Uz. He had a wife, seven grown-up sons, and three daughters. Job worshipped God and tried to please him. He had huge flocks and herds.

Job always made special sacrifices for his children just in case they had done something wrong, and he asked God to forgive them.

One day Satan, the evil tempter, told God he thought Job only obeyed God because God had made Job rich and given him a lovely family. God said, "Test him by taking away those things."

So Satan sent terrible trouble to Job. His oxen and donkeys were stolen. Fire burned up his sheep and their shepherds. Another tribe took his camels and killed their herdsmen. A terrible windstorm collapsed his oldest son's home, killing all of Job's children.

Job was heartbroken. But what he said was, "God gave me all I had and now God has taken it away. I still love him and praise him."

Then Satan said to God, "Well, Job is still faithful to you because he is healthy." So God said Satan could make Job ill. Big sores broke out all over Job's body.

129
Job's Friends

Job 2–37

When Job became sick, his wife asked him, "Why don't you curse God for letting all this happen to you?"

Job said, "God has given me many blessings. Why shouldn't I have trouble, too? Even if he killed me, I wouldn't curse him."

Three of Job's friends came to visit him. They said he was having so much trouble because he had sinned and offended God. "These troubles must be a punishment for disobeying God," they insisted. Day after day they sat and accused him of sinning.

"I really haven't done anything wrong," Job protested. "I've always tried to live in the right way and please God. And you aren't making me feel any better by saying all these things! A fine bunch of comforters you are!"

At last Job got tired of suffering, and he complained that God was being unfair to him. Then his friends said, "See, you are sinning! We said you must be doing something wrong!" And they argued with Job all the more.

130
God Blesses Job Again

Job 38–42

Finally God said, "That's enough! Job, let me ask you some questions. Where were you when I made the world? Can you possibly understand how wonderful my creation is?" And God described the animals and explained how he takes care of them. God said, "Do you think you are wise enough to do all of these things? You forget that you are just a man and I'm the great God of the universe!"

Job told God he was sorry for being so impatient and for not understanding God's ways. Job said, "Lord, now I really know you. I've seen how wonderful you are, and I despise myself.

I am so sorry I acted badly."

God also told Job's three friends that he was angry with them for saying such foolish things to Job when he was in trouble. God said, "Offer sacrifices to me, and my faithful servant Job will pray for you; then I will forgive you."

Then the Lord gave Job back his health and more riches than before. God even gave Job and his wife ten more children – seven sons and three daughters, the same number as before.

131
Jonah Disobeys God

Jonah 1

God chose Jonah to do a special job for him. God said, "I want you to travel to Nineveh and tell the people there that they are so wicked I'm going to destroy them."

Nineveh was a beautiful place, but the people were very evil. They did not love God, and they were terribly cruel to others.

Jonah knew that he might be killed if he went to Nineveh, so he decided he wouldn't deliver God's message. Instead, he went to the port of Joppa and bought a ticket to sail to Tarshish, across the Mediterranean Sea. He boarded the ship and fell asleep in the hold, thinking he was hiding from God.

A terrible storm came up suddenly, and the sailors were terrified. The captain found Jonah asleep and said, "Get up and pray to your God to save us."

Then the sailors tried to find out whose fault it was that they were in trouble. They decided it was Jonah's fault, and he knew they were right.

"Yes, you'd better throw me overboard. Then the storm will stop." Jonah knew what he had done!

132
Jonah and the Fish

Jonah 2–4

The sailors hated to throw Jonah into the sea, but it was either that or have their ship sink. They threw him overboard, and immediately the storm stopped. God sent an enormous fish, and when Jonah fell into the water, it swallowed him whole, without hurting him.

Jonah was alive inside the fish for three days and three nights. He was sorry about disobeying God. Jonah prayed, promising God he would do as God had said. God made the fish swim close to land and spit Jonah out. Jonah had another chance to preach to Nineveh, and this time he did it.

Jonah told the Ninevites, "God is going to destroy you because of your sin." Jonah was amazed that the king of Nineveh and his people believed him and were sorry for their wickedness. They asked God to forgive them and spare their lives, and God did.

Jonah was angry. He had wanted God to destroy the Ninevites because they were so cruel. Jonah was disappointed when they were forgiven. God scolded Jonah for having such an unforgiving attitude.

133
Hannah Prays for a Son

1 Samuel 1

Elkanah lived with his two wives, Hannah and Peninnah. He loved Hannah best, but she had no children, which made her very sad. Peninnah had several children. She made fun of Hannah and treated her unkindly.

Each year Elkanah took his family to the tabernacle at Shiloh to make his sacrifices and worship God. Year after year Peninnah would say cruel things to Hannah. Hannah was so unhappy that she couldn't eat or sleep, and she would cry bitterly because she was childless.

One evening while they were in Shiloh, Hannah went to the tabernacle to pray. She told the Lord about her sadness, and she promised that if he would give her a baby boy, she would let her son serve God in the tabernacle.

Eli, the high priest, watched her as she prayed. Because it looked as if she was muttering to herself, he thought she

had been drinking. He scolded her for being drunk, but she said, "No. I was just praying for something I want very much."

Then Eli said, "May God give you exactly what you prayed for!" Hannah went home feeling much better.

134
God Speaks to Samuel
1 Samuel 1–3

Hannah had a baby boy, whom she named Samuel. She didn't forget her promise to God. When Samuel was old enough, Hannah left him at the tabernacle to help Eli. Eli needed Samuel's help because Eli was very old.

Samuel's parents visited him each year. Hannah had three more sons and two daughters.

One night as Samuel lay in bed, he heard a voice calling his name. Samuel thought that it was Eli, so he went to see what Eli wanted. Eli told him he had not called. "Go back to bed," Eli said.

Again Samuel heard the voice calling him. Again he went to Eli and asked what he wanted.

"I didn't call you. Go back to bed, and next time you hear the voice, answer, 'Speak, Lord. I'm listening.'"

Samuel obeyed. When he heard the voice again, he said, "Yes, Lord. Speak, and I'll listen." God gave him a message for Eli about how he was going to punish Eli's disobedient sons, Hophni and Phinehas.

Samuel hated to give Eli such bad news, but he had to tell him.

135
Enemies Capture the Ark

1 Samuel 4

God often talked to Samuel. Samuel always listened, then told the people what God had said. Once the Israelites were fighting the Philistines. The Philistines were winning. The people had an idea. They would take the ark of the covenant with them into battle, and the ark would give them the victory. Hophni and Phinehas went into battle with the ark. But neither the people nor the priests had asked God's advice.

The Philistines were terrified when they heard about the ark because it represented God, and they thought the Israelites would win. So they fought harder and defeated the Israelites. Hophni and Phinehas were killed, and the Philistines captured the ark.

A young soldier ran to Shiloh. He told Eli, "Your two sons have been killed, and the Philistines have stolen the ark of the covenant."

When Eli heard the news, he fell over backward, broke his neck, and died. The Philistines took the ark to Ashdod and set it beside the idol of their god Dagon, in Dagon's temple.

136

God Brings the Ark Back

1 Samuel 5–7

In the morning the image of Dagon was lying on its face in front of the ark! The Philistines set it up again and went away. The next morning the idol was not only lying in front of the ark, but its head and hands had been broken off.

While the ark was there, God sent trouble to the Philistines. "We are being punished by the Israelites' God because we stole the ark. We have to get rid of it or we will all die!"

The leaders decided to send it to Gath. But when it got there, the people of Gath started dying too. They took it to another city, but when those people saw it coming, they said, "No!

Now we'll die too. Send it back to the Israelites or our whole nation will be destroyed."

The Philistines sent the ark back on a cart pulled by cows, and when the Israelites saw it coming, they were overcome with joy. But then they made a bad mistake. The Israelites opened the ark and looked inside, which was forbidden. A lot of them died as a result of that disobedience.

137
Israel Asks for a King
1 Samuel 7–8

The people of Israel wondered why they couldn't defeat the Philistines once and for all. Samuel told them it was because they had idols in their homes. He begged them to be sorry for their sin and to get rid of the idols, so they did. Then God gave them victory over the Philistines. Samuel led the people faithfully all of his life. When Samuel became old, he appointed his sons to be judges in his place. But Samuel's sons were dishonest and unfair. So the leaders of Israel said to Samuel, "You are too old to be our judge, and your sons are bad men. Find us a king to rule us."

Samuel didn't like the idea. He asked God what to do. God said, "Give them what they want. But warn them about what will happen if they have a king."

So Samuel warned the people, "You'll be sorry! A king will rule over you and take your money and the best of your crops and herds – even your sons and daughters. You will be like slaves."

But the people refused to listen. "We don't care. We want a king to help us defeat our enemies!"

138
God Chooses Saul to be King
1 Samuel 9–10

God promised to help Samuel find the right king. He said, "I'll send you a man from the tribe of Benjamin." Meanwhile, a handsome, young man named Saul was hunting for some lost donkeys.

After a long time Saul said to his servant, "We'd better give up and go home. My father will be worried about us."

His servant replied, "Let's just ask the man of God who lives here if he can help us."

So they went to the town where Samuel lived. Samuel saw them coming, and God told him, "That's the man to be king."

Samuel introduced himself to Saul and said, "Your father's donkeys have been found. Now, you are going to be very great in Israel!"

Saul said, "I'm from the smallest tribe, and my family isn't important. How can I be 'great'?"

Samuel explained to Saul that God had chosen him to be king. He poured oil over Saul's head, which showed that God had appointed him for a special service. Later Samuel announced to the country that Saul was to be their king, and all the people shouted, "Long live the king!"

139

Samuel Warns the People

1 Samuel 11–12

The Ammonite army attacked Jabesh-gilead, an Israelite city. When the elders of Jabesh asked for a peace treaty, the Ammonite general said, "I'll make peace with you – but I'll put out every man's right eye!"

The elders sent messengers to beg all the other Israelites for help. When Saul heard the Ammonites' threat, the Spirit of God came upon him. In anger he killed two oxen, cut them up, and sent a piece to each of Israel's tribes with a message. "This is what I'll do to all your oxen if you don't come and help the people of Jabesh!"

The tribes sent soldiers in a hurry, and Saul led them into battle where they defeated the Ammonites. Then Samuel spoke to the people. "I've given you the king you wanted. And I've been your leader since I was a child. I have never been selfish or dishonest."

Then Samuel reminded them that they had sinned by insisting upon having a king. To prove it, he asked God to send a sign – a thunderstorm that frightened them. Samuel said, "God will reward you if you obey him but punish you if you don't."

140
Saul Disobeys the Lord

1 Samuel 13

Saul attacked a Philistine outpost at Geba. When the news reached the rest of the Philistines, they got together their huge army and marched against Israel. The Israelites were terrified. They didn't have the forces to fight such a vast army. They ran away and hid. Some even crossed the Jordan River to get away from the Philistines.

Saul and some of the soldiers waited at Gilgal because Samuel had told him he would come there in seven days to make sacrifices and ask for God's advice. When Samuel didn't come on time, Saul decided to make the sacrifices himself, though he had no right to do that.

Just as Saul finished the offering, Samuel arrived and asked, "What do you think you're doing?"

"You didn't come when you promised, and our enemies are about to kill us. I thought I'd better make the burnt offering myself."

Samuel shouted, "That was stupid! If you had done the right thing, God would have let you and your family be kings forever. But now God is going to take away the kingdom and give it to someone who will be obedient!"

141
Jonathan Frightens an Army

1 Samuel 14

Saul's son, Jonathan, said to his armour bearer, "Let's sneak across to the Philistine camp. The Lord might do

some kind of miracle and let us get rid of the Philistines! When they see us, if they call, 'Get away from here or we'll kill you!' then we'll stop. But if they say, 'Come up here and fight with us!' we'll know that God's going to help us win."

When the Philistine soldiers saw the two men, they yelled, "Look! The Israelites are crawling out of their holes! Come on up here, and we'll give you a fight!"

Jonathan and his friend climbed up and started fighting. They killed about twenty men, and the other soldiers became afraid. Soon the whole army was in complete panic. Then God sent an earthquake. The Philistine soldiers were so confused that they started killing each other as they tried to run away!

In the Israelite camp, Saul's sentries could see that the Philistines were disappearing, so the Israelite soldiers

came out of hiding and ran after them – and God gave them a great victory.

142
David to Be the Next King
1 Samuel 15–16

Saul felt terrible when he heard that because of his sin God was going to give Israel a new king. He grabbed Samuel's robe, and it tore. Samuel said, "That's the way the kingdom is going to be torn out of your hands!"

Saul and Samuel worshipped together one more time, then went to their homes, never to see one another again.

God told Samuel to go to Bethlehem and see Jesse. "One of his sons is to be the next king. Invite Jesse to worship with you."

Samuel looked carefully at Jesse's sons when they came with their father to worship. They were all fine, strong men, but God told Samuel, "None of these is the one I've chosen. I don't choose people because of the way they look. I decide because of what's in their hearts."

Samuel asked Jesse if he had any other sons. Jesse said, "Only David, my youngest."

"Call him," Samuel ordered. David came in, a handsome young fellow.

"That's the one!" God said to Samuel. Samuel poured oil on David's head, showing everyone that he was to be the next king. And God sent his Spirit into David's heart.

143
David Plays for King Saul
1 Samuel 16

Saul proved to be a disobedient king, so God took his Spirit away from Saul and allowed a bad, tormenting spirit to come into his heart, which made Saul nervous, sad, and fearful.

Saul's advisors suggested that music might make him feel better. And Saul liked that idea.

One of the servants said, "David, one of Jesse's sons, plays the harp beautifully. He learned to play out in the fields while he was watching his father's flock of sheep. He's a good musician, and the Lord is with him."

Saul asked Jesse to send David. Jesse sent David to Saul, along with a lot of gifts. Saul liked David from the start and appointed him to be his personal musician. Each time Saul felt the evil spirit coming into his heart, he asked David to play the harp. The music would calm Saul down

and the troublesome spirit would leave him for a while. When Saul didn't need him, David would spend time helping Jesse with the sheep, and Saul would almost forget about him.

144

Goliath Frightens the Israelites

1 Samuel 17

The Philistines decided to attack again, so the two armies got ready for war. The Philistines were in the hills on one side of a valley, and the Israelite army was on the other side of the valley.

The Philistines had a giant in their army – he was more than nine feet tall. The giant named Goliath was amazingly strong. He wore metal armour that weighed over one hundred pounds! He carried a big, thick spear with a fifteen pound tip. Another soldier walked in front of him, carrying a big shield to protect him.

Goliath wasn't afraid of anybody. He laughed at the Israelite soldiers. He shouted, "You don't all need to get killed. Send out just one soldier to fight with me. If he can kill me, the Philistines will be your servants. But if I kill him, then you will have to serve us! Come on, isn't anyone brave enough to fight me?"

Saul was afraid of Goliath, and so were all of his soldiers. No one had the courage to walk out into the valley and tangle with a giant! So they stayed in their camp while Goliath kept daring them to fight.

145

David Hears Goliath's Challenge

1 Samuel 17

David's older brothers were among Saul's soldiers. One day Jesse sent David to the battlefield to take some food to his brothers and to find out how they were doing. David found his brothers, and as they were talking, Goliath shouted out his daily challenge.

When David heard this, he asked the Israelite soldiers, "Who is this fellow who dares to talk like that to the army of the living God?"

The soldiers explained, and they told David that whoever killed Goliath would receive a big reward and would be allowed to marry Saul's daughter. Some of the men told Saul what David had said, so Saul sent for him.

"I'll kill Goliath for you," David said to the king.

"No!" said Saul. "You're just a young man, and that giant has been a warrior all his life."

David said, "And I've been a shepherd all my life. God has given me strength to kill wild animals that were trying to attack my sheep. I've killed a lion and a bear with my bare hands! The same God will help me kill this giant."

146

David Kills Goliath

1 Samuel 17

When Saul saw how brave David was, he said, "Go ahead – and God bless you." Saul offered his armour to David, but it was far too big and heavy for David, so he didn't wear it.

David picked up five smooth stones. With his slingshot in his hand, he walked out to meet Goliath. The giant took one look at David and roared, "Why, you're just a boy! Come on out here, and I'll feed you to the vultures!"

David called, "You are depending on your weapons, but I'm depending on the Lord. I will kill you and cut off your head, and everyone will know it was because of my God's power."

Then David ran toward Goliath, swinging his sling. David let a stone fly. It hit the giant in the forehead, and David used Goliath's sword to cut off his head.

When the Philistines saw their greatest warrior fall dead, they ran away. The Israelite soldiers chased them back into their own territory, killing many of them.

Saul made David an officer in his army.

147
Saul is Jealous
1 Samuel 18

David became a great hero after he killed Goliath and a very successful soldier in Saul's army. Saul was jealous because David was so popular. Saul worried that David would take the kingdom away from him.

The next day the evil spirit came back and bothered Saul again. David began to play the harp to try to quiet Saul, but Saul threw a spear at David. David dodged it. This happened again, but again David jumped aside,

and the spear missed him.

Saul thought he would send David to fight the Philistines, then maybe David would be killed. Saul said, "I promised you my oldest daughter for killing Goliath, but first you must go out and win a battle." While David was out fighting, Saul gave that daughter in marriage to another man.

David came back unharmed. He and another of Saul's daughters, Michal, wanted to get married, but Saul said, "No, first you must kill one hundred Philistines." David went out and killed two hundred of them, so Saul had to let Michal marry him. And the people loved David more and more.

148
David's Best Friend
1 Samuel 18; 20

David and Saul's son, Jonathan, became the best of friends. David asked Jonathan why the king wanted to kill him. Jonathan replied, "I don't think he would kill you – but I'll find out and let you know."

David said, "King Saul would like to see me dead. Tomorrow is the feast of the new moon. I'll stay away from the court, and you can find out what your father thinks of me."

"All right," Jonathan answered. "If he's as angry as you think, I'll come out here and shoot some arrows into the field. I'll call to my helper, 'The arrows are farther out in the field.' Then you will know you are in danger."

As they parted, David and Jonathan made a promise that they would always take care of each other's families.

At the feast, Jonathan found out that his father was really jealous enough to kill David, so Jonathan went out to the field and gave the signal he and David had agreed upon. David sadly said goodbye and left to escape from Saul.

— 149 —
David Tells a Lie
1 Samuel 21

David left Saul's court so quickly that he didn't take his weapons or any food with him. He went to Nob, where the ark of the covenant was being kept, and visited Ahimelech, the priest. David lied to Ahimelech. He said, "Saul has sent me on a secret mission. I need some supplies for my men who are waiting nearby. Do you have any bread?"

Ahimelech answered, "I don't have any regular bread, but I can give you some of the special bread from the altar if you and your men have been obeying the Law."

"Yes, we have," said David. "And do you have a sword I may use? My business for the king made me leave so quickly that I couldn't bring my own."

"The only sword here is the one that belonged to Goliath. You could take that."

Doeg, Saul's head herdsman, overheard David's conversation with Ahimelech. He hurried back to Saul's court and told him he had seen David at Nob, talking to the priest.

— 150 —
The Result of the Lie
1 Samuel 22

When Doeg told Saul what he had seen at Nob, Saul was furious and blamed Ahimelech for helping David. He sent for Ahimelech and the other priests. He yelled at Ahimelech for helping David escape and giving him supplies. Ahimelech said, "I didn't know he was lying to me. I thought I was doing the right thing to help the king's son-in-law."

The king roared at him, "Don't make excuses! You will die – you and all your family and the other priests too." Saul ordered his soldiers to kill the priests, but they were afraid to harm God's appointed priests, so they refused.

Then Saul ordered Doeg to do it, and Doeg obeyed. He killed eighty-five priests, then went to Nob and killed Ahimelech's relatives and his livestock. Only one son, Abiathar, escaped. He found David and told him what had happened to Ahimelech and the other priests.

David was heartbroken to think that his selfish lie had caused such terrible trouble. He was sorry he had not trusted God to take care of him instead of lying to protect himself.

151
David Spares Saul's Life

1 Samuel 23–24

David had about four hundred followers. When he heard that the Philistines were causing trouble again, he asked God if he should fight them. God said yes, so they had a battle at Keilah. David's men won.

When Saul heard about it, he said, "Now I can catch David while he's in Keilah." David heard that Saul was coming after him, and David asked the Lord whether he was in danger. The Lord said he was, so David and his army left the city and travelled around, hiding wherever they could.

From then on, Saul kept trying to find David so he could kill him. But God always warned David in time. More than once David had a chance to kill Saul, but David wouldn't do it, even when his own men said he should.

"No," David said, "it would be wrong for me to harm the man God has chosen as king."

Once David and his men found Saul and his soldiers sleeping in a cave. David crept up quietly and cut off a bit of Saul's robe without waking him. But he would never hurt the king.

152
Nabal Insults David

1 Samuel 25

For a while David and his men lived in a desert area where there was a rich sheep owner named Nabal. David's soldiers were friendly with Nabal's shepherds and were careful never to steal any of Nabal's sheep. Once David sent this message to Nabal: "We are in need of some supplies, for it is a feast time for us. Would you be so kind as to give us whatever food you can spare?"

Nabal was a mean, unpleasant man, and he answered crossly, "Why should I give my valuable food to someone who may be a runaway or a criminal for all I know? Forget it!"

This answer made David angry, so he went to teach Nabal a lesson. Meanwhile, one of Nabal's shepherds hurried to Nabal's wife, Abigail, who was gentle and kind and very beautiful. He told her how kind David's men had been to them and how rude Nabal had been to David's messenger.

Abigail realized they were in danger because of Nabal's insults, so she thought of a plan. Could she save them from David's anger?

153
David Marries Abigail

1 Samuel 25

Abigail prepared some food for David and his men –bread, wine, sheep ready for cooking, roasted grain, and cakes of raisins and dried figs. She loaded it all onto donkeys and sent servants on ahead. Abigail followed.

Abigail met David as he approached Nabal's farm. She bowed low before him.

She said, "Sir, I apologize for my husband's rudeness. He is a wicked, foolish man. Please forgive us and accept this food. I know God has blessed you and will make you the king of Israel. Surely you would not want to have Nabal's death on your conscience."

David's heart was touched, and he answered, "Of course I accept your apology. Thank you for your gift. Go back home in peace."

Abigail went home, and the next day she told Nabal how she had prevented David from killing him. Nabal was so shocked that he became very ill and couldn't move. Ten days later, he died.

When David heard that Nabal was dead, he sent his men to bring Abigail to his camp, and they were married.

154
David Refuses to Kill the King

1 Samuel 26

Once when Saul was looking for him, David and his nephew Abishai crept over to Saul's camp at night. Saul was asleep, with Abner, his general, beside him. The other soldiers lay around them, to protect them. Saul's spear was stuck into the ground beside his head. Abishai whispered to David, "God has given us a good chance to get rid of your enemy."

"No!" David answered. "God made him king, and it would be wrong to kill him. Just take his spear and water bottle, and let's get out of here."

No one saw them or heard them. When they were a safe distance away,

David shouted, "Hey, Abner! Wake up! You haven't been taking very good care of the king. Where are his spear and his water jar?"

Saul recognized David's voice, and he called, "Is that you, David?"

"Yes, my lord. Tell me what I've done to deserve your anger. I would never hurt you."

Then Saul told David he was sorry. Saul said, "Come on home now, and I won't hurt you." But David didn't trust Saul, so David went away and Saul went home.

155
Saul Calls Samuel's Spirit

1 Samuel 28

David realized that Saul might chase him forever, so he asked Achish, a Philistine leader, for a city to live in. In return, he would help Achish with his wars. David, his men, and their families settled in the city of Ziklag.

After a while some of the Philistines prepared to attack Saul's army. Saul asked God what to do but got no answer. Saul used to get advice from the Lord through Samuel, but Samuel had died. Saul wanted to try to talk to Samuel's spirit, but he himself had made a law against trying to get messages from the dead. He was so desperate that he disguised himself and went to Endor, where there was a woman who thought she could talk to dead people.

Even she was surprised when Samuel appeared! Then she guessed that her visitor was the king, and she was terrified.

Saul asked Samuel what he should do about the Philistines. Samuel said, "You got yourself into this when you disobeyed God. Now God will give David the kingdom. And when you fight with the Philistines, they will win. Tomorrow you will be dead."

156
David Defeats the Amalekites

1 Samuel 29–30

David and his men expected to fight with the Philistines against Saul's army. But some of the Philistine leaders didn't trust David. "He'll probably change sides when we start fighting." So David took his men back to Ziklag, only to find that the Amalekite army had burned the city and had taken the women and children – including David's two wives.

David asked God, "If I catch up with the Amalekites, can I defeat them and get our families back?"

God said, "Yes, go! You will get back everything they have stolen."

So David and his men started out. Some of the soldiers stayed behind. The rest of them soon caught up to the Amalekites and fought fiercely with them. At last David and his men killed almost all the enemy and were able to take their wives and children and property home.

When they rejoined the soldiers who had stayed behind, some of David's men said, "They don't deserve any of the loot because they didn't help with the fighting."

David said, "No, that's not fair, and after all, the Lord is the one who gives us the victory!"

— 157 —
Israel's First King Dies

1 Samuel 31

The Philistines overpowered the Israelites and killed many of them, including Saul's sons. Saul was wounded very badly. He said to his armour bearer, "Please kill me so that the Philistines won't capture me and torture me."

But his armour bearer couldn't do it, so Saul took his own life by making himself fall against the point of his sword. The Philistines chased the Israelites out of their towns and occupied them.

When the Philistine soldiers went out onto the battlefield to steal things from the bodies of the dead soldiers, they found the bodies of Saul and his sons. The Philistines cut off their heads and displayed them on the wall of one of their cities to show their disrespect for the Israelite king.

When the Israelites heard that, they came and took away the bodies. The Israelites cremated them and buried the ashes; then they mourned for their king for seven days.

158
David is Crowned King

2 Samuel 1–4

David was sorry when he heard that Saul and Jonathan were dead. David asked God, "Should I move back to Judah?" and God said yes. So David and his men and their families settled in the city of Hebron. The leaders of Judah crowned David king of their tribe.

Meanwhile, Saul's army commander, Abner, chose Saul's son Ishbosheth to be king of the other tribes of Israel. So God's people were divided into two groups, each with its own king. For years they fought, each trying to take control of the whole nation.

Gradually David's group became the stronger. Abner and Ishbosheth quarrelled, and Abner offered to surrender Israel's forces to David in exchange for being made commander of the combined army.

Joab, one of David's chief soldiers, hated Abner, so without David's knowing it, he murdered Abner. Then Ishbosheth was killed by two of his army captains. They bragged about it to David. David was angry. He had wanted always to be fair to Saul's family, so David had the assassins killed.

159
God Punishes Uzzah

2 Samuel 5–6

With the army of Israel united and strong, David drove the Jebusites out of Jerusalem. Then he made it his capital city. Next, David defeated the Philistines.

David wanted the ark back where it belonged, so he went to the town where it had been held for many years. The ark was placed on a new oxcart, and two men, Uzzah and Ahio, walked beside it. When one of the oxen stumbled, Uzzah put out his hand and held the ark steady.

God had said that men must never touch the ark. They must move it by lifting it with poles. So when Uzzah touched the ark, God was angry with Uzzah and struck him dead. David said, "I'm afraid to keep on moving the ark. We'll leave it here, at the home of Obed-edom."

The ark was there for three months, and during that time God greatly blessed Obed-edom and his family. When David saw this, he decided it was time to go back and get the ark and take it home.

160
The Ark Returns to Jerusalem

2 Samuel 6

David went to the home of Obed-edom and got the ark. He and the people with him started the trip to Jerusalem. They were so happy that they sang and danced and shouted for joy as they travelled along.

As they entered Jerusalem, David danced and sang more than anyone else. His wife

Michal, Saul's daughter, watched the procession from the window. She thought the way David was acting was disgusting.

At last the ark was back where it belonged, and David made more sacrifices. Then he blessed the people in the name of the Lord and gave everyone a gift of bread, raisins, and dates.

David went home to give blessings to his own family. But Michal didn't feel like celebrating. She said, "You really made a fool of yourself today, jumping around without your royal robe – in public!"

David replied, "Look, I was dancing before the Lord, not to get the attention of people. God chose me to be king. I would be willing to look even more foolish than I did today to express my thanks to God!"

— 161 —
David's Kindness to Jonathan's Family

2 Samuel 9

David missed Jonathan and wanted to do something to honour his memory. He remembered how he and Jonathan had promised to take care of each other's families if either of them should die. David sent for Ziba, an old servant of Saul's, and asked him if any members of Saul's household were still alive.

The servant said, "Yes, one of Jonathan's sons is alive. He is Mephibosheth, who was crippled when he was a little boy."

So David sent for Mephibosheth. "Don't be afraid of me," David said. "I loved your father, Jonathan, and I want to be kind to you for his sake. I'll give

back your family's land, but I want you to come and live here at the palace with me."

Then David said to Ziba, "I've given all of Saul's land to Mephibosheth. I want you and your family to farm Mephibosheth's land so his family will have plenty of food. But he is going to live at the palace as my guest for the rest of his life."

— 162 —
David and Bathsheba

2 Samuel 11

David's army was at war with the Ammonites, but David stayed in Jerusalem. One night as he walked around on the palace roof David saw, in a nearby home, a beautiful woman bathing. She was Bathsheba, the wife of Uriah, one of David's army officers.

David sent for her and slept with her as if she were his wife. She became pregnant.

David didn't want anyone to know he was the baby's father. He told Uriah to go home so that it would look as if

Uriah had been with his wife and the baby was his. But Uriah refused. He said, "My duty is to stay with the army."

David decided to get rid of Uriah so that he could marry Bathsheba. David told General Joab to send Uriah into a part of the fighting where he would almost certainly be killed. So Joab put Uriah on the front line and then pulled the other soldiers back, leaving Uriah to die. Joab sent the news of his death to David.

David married Bathsheba, and soon she had a baby boy.

163
The Baby Dies

2 Samuel 12

God was angry with David because he had committed adultery and murder. He sent a prophet named Nathan to David. Nathan told David this story: "Once two men were neighbours. One was very rich and had many sheep and cattle. The other was poor; he had only one little ewe lamb, which was almost like one of the family. Once the rich man had a guest. Instead of killing one of his own sheep, he stole the poor man's lamb and cooked it for his guest's dinner."

David was terribly angry. He said, "Why, a selfish man like that should be killed."

Nathan said, "David, you are that rich man. God has been good to you. He made you king over Israel and Judah. You have everything you need, yet you have stolen Uriah's wife and then murdered him."

David confessed that he had sinned against God. Nathan said that because he was sorry, he would not have to die, but Bathsheba's baby would die. In a few days the baby became very sick, and although David prayed for him, the baby died.

164
A Rebellious Son

2 Samuel 13–15

David had married several women, so he had children who were half-brothers and half-sisters. Some of them were jealous of one another and quarrelled a lot. Once David's oldest son, Amnon, hurt the sister of his half-brother Absalom. Absalom was furious. He told his servants to kill Amnon – which was as bad as doing the killing himself. Absalom had to run away to keep David from punishing him, and he stayed away for three years.

David had been angry with Absalom, but he missed his son. Joab persuaded him to allow Absalom to return home.

Absalom lived in Jerusalem for two years, but his father refused to see him. Finally Absalom asked Joab to get David to change his mind. So David let Absalom come and see him.

This did not heal the trouble between them. Absalom didn't forgive his father for not accepting him. He decided to try to get the kingdom away from David. He was a fine-looking young man, with long thick hair that he cut only once a year. People liked him, and he went to Hebron and gathered a lot of followers.

165

David Runs Away from His Son

2 Samuel 15–17

When David realized how popular Absalom had become, he thought, "I'd better get out of Jerusalem before he comes after me to kill me." David's friend Hushai wanted to go with him, but David asked him to stay and send him news of what Absalom was doing. So Hushai stayed, but David and his soldiers hid in the wilderness.

Soon afterward, Absalom and his army entered the city. His advisor said, "Let's chase after David and kill him. Then the people will make you king in his place."

Hushai pretended to be loyal to Absalom, so Absalom asked Hushai what he thought. Hushai said, "You had better wait and gather a much larger army." He said this to give David more time to escape. Then he sent a message to David, telling him what Absalom was planning.

Some of Absalom's spies saw the messengers and chased them. But a man hid them in his well until the spies gave up looking for them. Then the messengers went on and warned David to get ready for war.

166
Absalom Hangs by His Hair

2 Samuel 18

David divided his army into three groups, each under one of his generals. As the soldiers marched out to battle, David said to the three generals, Joab, Abishai, and Ittai, "Please be gentle with my son Absalom." And all the soldiers heard what David said to the generals. The two armies fought in a forest, and David's forces won. Twenty thousand men were killed. As Absalom was riding away from the battlefield, his long hair got caught in the branches of an oak tree, and he was left hanging there by his hair. One of David's soldiers saw him and told Joab.

Joab said, "Why didn't you kill him when you had the chance?"

The soldier said, "I wouldn't harm him because I heard what King David said to you and the other generals about being merciful to Absalom."

Joab said, "Well, I don't mind doing it." He rode back to the tree where Absalom was hanging and stabbed him with daggers. And so the rebellion against King David ended.

167
King David Praises God

2 Samuel 18–23

David loved Absalom and was sad when he got killed. He made everyone else feel sad, too, instead of being joyful about their victory. Joab said to David, "Your people have fought bravely to save you from that traitor Absalom. Now you are behaving as if they had done something wrong. If you want them to be loyal to you, you had better stop this and congratulate them." So David stopped mourning and went out to thank his army.

Then Sheba, another rebel, came along and got Israel to follow him. The people of Judah stayed loyal to David. After more fighting, Sheba was killed and his rebellion stopped.

At last the nation was united. David had many strong, faithful warriors who helped defeat Israel's enemies. When David grew too old to fight, his warriors protected him.

In his old age David made up songs of praise to God, just as he had done when he was a young shepherd boy. Many of David's songs are in the Bible, in the book of Psalms.

168
David Chooses Solomon to Be King
1 Kings 1–2

David had several sons, and he had to decide who would be king after him. One son, Adonijah, tried to force the people to accept him as king. Bathsheba went to David and said, "You told me that my son Solomon was to be the king after you die. Adonijah has persuaded the people to crown him without your knowing about it. What are you going to do about this?"

The prophet Nathan came to see David, too, and he urged David to make Solomon king right away. David told Nathan and the priests to anoint Solomon and to announce to all the country that he was the new king.

When Adonijah heard the news, he was afraid Solomon would kill him as punishment for trying to get the kingdom. He went to the tabernacle and took hold of the horns of the altar for protection. Solomon said, "Tell Adonijah that if he will be a good man, I won't harm him. But if he gets into trouble, he shall die."

David talked with Solomon and told him many things he needed to know to be a good king.

— 169 —
Solomon Becomes King

1 Kings 2

King David died. He had been king for forty years. Now Solomon was the king, and he tried to rule wisely. After Solomon became king, Adonijah wanted to marry Abishag, who had nursed David during the last years of his life. Adonijah asked Bathsheba to get Solomon's permission.

Solomon said, "Certainly not. And I vow that even today I will see that Adonijah is killed!" And he ordered Benaiah to kill Adonijah.

Solomon didn't trust Abiathar the priest, but he didn't want to kill him because of Abiathar's faithfulness to King David. So he told him he could no longer be a priest, and that he had to return to his boyhood home.

Joab had helped Adonijah try to become king. When Joab heard about Adonijah's death and Abiathar's exile, he thought he would probably be next. Joab went to the tabernacle and held the horns of the altar for safety, but Solomon had him killed anyway because of his rebellion. Then no one was left who wanted to rebel against Solomon.

— 170 —
Solomon Makes a Wise Decision

1 Kings 3

In a dream one night, Solomon told God he wanted wisdom more than anything else. God said, "I am going to give you wisdom, and riches and honour too, even though you didn't ask for them."

One day two women came to ask Solomon to settle a quarrel.

One said, "This other woman and I each had a baby. Her baby died, but in the night she took my baby and left her dead baby in my bed. I knew that the dead child was hers, but she wouldn't give back my baby."

The other woman said, "That's not true! The dead baby is hers, and the living baby is mine."

Solomon tested them. He took a sword, held up the living baby, and said, "We'll cut the baby in two and give half to each woman."

One of the women agreed, but the real mother cried out, "No! Give him to her! I'd rather give him up than let him be killed."

Then Solomon said, "Give the baby to the one who wants his life spared. She is the real mother."

Everyone could see how wise God had made Solomon.

171
Solomon Builds God's Temple

1 Kings 5–7; 9

Solomon was eager to build a temple as a permanent house for God. King Hiram of Tyre offered to help. He sent beautiful cedar and cypress logs, and Solomon paid him by providing food for his workmen. Solomon sent men to help with the logging while others cut big blocks of stone from quarries.

After they had prepared all the materials, the building began. All the stone had been cut to the right size at the quarry. The inside of the walls was lined with the cedar boards; then everything was covered with gold – even the ceiling and the cypress floors were bright gold.

Like the tabernacle, the Temple had a special inner room called the Most Holy Place. Everything in the room was covered with pure gold. There the ark was kept, and the gold-covered altar. Beside the ark were two very large carved figures of cherubs.

The Temple was a beautiful house for God. The Lord said to Solomon, "As long as you obey me and live as you should, I will live here among your people and will never abandon you."

172
God's Glory Fills the Temple

1 Kings 7–8

Next, all the furnishings for the Temple were made. Skilful craftsmen made basins, pots, shovels, tanks, latticework, and pillars. They did beautiful carving in the wood panelling, then overlaid it with gold. Everything was made as perfectly as possible because it was for the house of God.

After seven years, everything was finished. Solomon called the people together for a big celebration. The priests carried the ark from the tabernacle and placed it in the Most Holy Place, with the wings of the two large cherubs shadowing its cover. As the

priests came out of the Most Holy Place, the glory of God came and filled the Temple like a huge cloud.

King Solomon blessed the people and then prayed. He dedicated the Temple to God's service and promised that he and his people would always worship God faithfully.

Then he sacrificed thousands of animals as a peace offering. He and the people celebrated for fourteen days. Their hearts were full of joy and thanksgiving for God's blessings to them.

173

Solomon's Great Kingdom

1 Kings 10

Solomon's riches and the beauty of the Temple and of his palace were famous all over the world. Much of his wealth came from taxes and money earned from trade with other countries. He ate from solid-gold dishes, and his throne was made of ivory, all covered with gold. He owned many thousands of horses, with fourteen hundred chariots and twelve thousand horses.

Because God had given Solomon great wisdom, people came to him from all over the world to ask for his advice about their problems. They brought him expensive gifts in appreciation for his help. The queen of Sheba came to visit Solomon because she was curious about all the reports of his wealth and wisdom. She brought him many gifts, and he gave her a tour of his palace and all his possessions.

She asked Solomon hard questions, and he was able to answer them all. She was amazed by everything she saw, as well as by his God-given wisdom.

174

King Solomon Breaks God's Law

1 Kings 11

King Solomon made a mistake. He married the wrong kind of women. His first wife was the daughter of Pharaoh. After that he married hundreds of women, and most of them came from countries and tribes where the people worshipped idols. His wives were idol-worshippers, so Solomon built places for them to worship their false gods. After a while he himself began to believe in these gods and worship them.

This was a great sin, and God was disappointed in Solomon.

God spoke sternly to Solomon: "You told me you would always obey me, and you said you would lead the people to worship only me. You have broken your word, so I will take away most of the kingdom from your family. Because I loved your father, David, I will let you go on being king as long as you live. But after you die, all but one tribe will rebel against your son."

And that was the end of Solomon's

peaceful years. Enemies began to attack him, and the rest of his life was full of trouble and warfare.

175
The Kingdom is Divided

1 Kings 11–12

Ahijah, a prophet, met Jeroboam, one of Solomon's officials. Ahijah took off his coat and tore it into twelve pieces. Ahijah handed ten pieces to Jeroboam and said, "The Lord is going to make you the king of ten tribes of Israel. Only the tribes of Judah and Benjamin will stay in Solomon's family after his death."

Solomon heard about this and tried to kill Jeroboam. But Jeroboam escaped.

After Solomon had been king for forty years, he died. His son Rehoboam became king.

Jeroboam returned for the ceremony. He made trouble for Rehoboam by getting some people to ask the new king, "Are you going to be as hard on us as Solomon was, or will you be more kind?"

Rehoboam wasn't sure how to answer, so he asked for advice. Older people told him to answer pleasantly, but young men advised him to get tough. Rehoboam took the young men's advice, and this made the people angry.

They said, "We don't want this mean fellow to be our king. Let Rehoboam rule his own little family tribe. We'll get Jeroboam to rule the rest of the country." This was just what God had planned.

176
Jeroboam Builds Idols

1 Kings 12–13

God's people were divided into two different nations: Israel was ruled by Jeroboam and Judah by Rehoboam.

Rehoboam thought he should fight to reunite the kingdom, but God said no.

Jeroboam set up his capital at Shechem. He thought, "If my people go to the Temple in Jerusalem, they may want to be part of Judah and give their loyalty to Rehoboam. I'd better make them a place to worship here in Israel."

Then he committed a great sin. He formed two golden calves and set up one in Dan and the other in Bethel.

He made shrines all over the countryside and appointed new priests who were not Levites. He also set new times for feasts and festivals, ignoring the rules God had given the people for proper worship.

God sent a prophet from Judah to Jeroboam, who was making an offering.

The prophet said, "One of the kings of Judah will kill these false priests. To prove it, God will split this altar in two."

Jeroboam was angry. He pointed to the prophet and yelled, "Grab him!" Instantly the king's hand was paralyzed, and the altar split in two.

177
A Lion Kills a Prophet
1 Kings 13

Jeroboam begged the prophet to pray for him. The prophet asked God to heal Jeroboam, and immediately his hand was all right. Jeroboam invited the prophet to eat at his home. The prophet said, "No, God told me I must not eat or drink anything here." He started back to Judah.

Another old prophet lived in Bethel. He heard about the prophet from Judah and what had happened to Jeroboam. He rode after the prophet from Judah and invited him home for a meal. The prophet from Judah refused: "God has forbidden me to eat or drink anything in Israel."

Then the old prophet lied. He said, "I am a prophet, and God told me it would be all right."

The prophet from Judah believed him and went to the old prophet's home and had a meal. Then the Lord gave the old prophet this message for the prophet from Judah: "You have disobeyed me. Therefore your body will not be buried with your ancestors." The prophet from Judah started for home again. But a lion killed him along the road. His body was taken back to Bethel and buried, far away from his family burial place.

178
Jeroboam's Son Dies

1 Kings 14

Jeroboam had a little boy named Abijah, who became very sick. Jeroboam told his wife, "Go in disguise to the prophet, Ahijah, who told me I would be king. Ask him what will happen to our son."

His wife obeyed. She took gifts of food to Ahijah, who by this time was very old and blind.

Before she got there, the Lord told Ahijah she was coming. And the Lord told Ahijah how to answer her. When the old man heard her at his door, he called, "Come on in, wife of Jeroboam!

Why are you trying to fool me?"

Then he gave her this message: "Tell Jeroboam that the Lord took the kingdom away from David's family and made him king. But Jeroboam has disobeyed the Lord by making idols for the people to worship. As his punishment, your little boy is going to die." Ahijah then told the queen, "Go on home. As soon as you get there, your little son will die." And that is what happened.

Jeroboam ruled for twenty-two years. When he died, his son Nadab became king.

179
More Wicked Kings

1 Kings 15–16

During the next forty years, Israel had one king after another, and they did many things that displeased God. Nadab ruled Israel for only two years. He led the people in worshipping the golden calves his father, Jeroboam, had made. Then Baasha wanted the throne, so he killed Nadab and became king. As soon as his reign began, he killed every one of Jeroboam's family.

Baasha was an idol-worshipper too. After he had been king for twenty-four years, he died and his son Elah became king.

Elah was a bad king, but he ruled for only two years. Zimri assassinated him and took the throne while many of the men of Israel were away fighting the Philistines. When the army of Israel heard the news, they said, "Let's get rid of Zimri right away! We want Omri."

They marched to the city where Zimri had his palace. He shut himself into his palace and set fire to it, committing suicide before the soldiers could kill him.

Omri established the capital of Israel at Samaria. He wasn't a good king either. He worshipped the golden calves and turned his back on the Lord God. He ruled for twelve years, and after his death his son Ahab was crowned king.

180
Miracle Food

1 Kings 16–17

From Jeroboam to Omri, Israel had seven kings, and not one of them loved and obeyed God. All of them bowed down to idols and worshipped false gods. Ahab was the worst king of all! He married Jezebel, the daughter of a heathen king. She worshipped the false god Baal, and soon Ahab began to worship him too. He built a temple to Baal and set up altars for idol worship.

God sent the prophet Elijah to tell Ahab about the punishment God would send. The message was this: "My God says that for the next few years, no rain will fall unless I give my permission."

Ahab was furious with Elijah, so God told Elijah to hurry away and hide near Kerith Brook. "You can drink the water from the brook, and I will send ravens to bring you food."

For a long time Elijah ate the bread and meat the ravens brought and had water to drink from the brook. But without rain, the brook finally dried up, so God said, "Now go to the village of Zarephath. I have told a widow there to take care of you."

— 181 —
Elijah Raises a Dead Boy to Life

1 Kings 17

As Elijah entered Zarephath, he saw a woman picking up sticks. He said, "May I please have a drink of water and some bread?" She shook her head sadly. "I don't have any bread – just a handful of flour and a few drops of oil. I am going to make a fire and bake a last loaf for my son and myself. Then we will starve to death."

Elijah said, "Don't worry! Bake the loaf, and give me some. God has promised that your flour and oil will not run out until the rain comes and there are crops again."

The widow baked bread and gave Elijah some. From then on, until the drought was over, she always had enough food for herself, her son, and Elijah.

One day her son got sick and died. She was heartbroken. Elijah prayed, "Lord, this woman has helped me. Why have you let her boy die?"

Three times Elijah cried out to God, "Please give back this child's life!" And the boy came back to life!

Elijah took him to his mother and said, "Look! He's alive again!"

The woman said, "You really are a man of God, and everything God tells you to say is true."

182
Drought and Famine
1 Kings 18

After three more years of drought, God told Elijah to go to King Ahab and tell him God was going to end the drought. Meanwhile, the king and Obadiah, one of his officers, went out to look for some grass for their horses and mules. The king said, "Let's separate. We must find food to save these animals from starvation."

Obadiah met Elijah and recognized him. Elijah said, "I'm on my way to the palace to see Ahab. Please tell him I am coming."

"I can't," Obadiah groaned. "The king has been looking for you everywhere. If I tell him you are coming and God sends you somewhere else, he will be furious. He'll probably kill me!"

Elijah said, "Don't worry. I won't disappear again." When Ahab heard that Elijah was coming, he went out to meet him. He yelled, "So, there you are, you troublemaker."

Elijah answered, "No! You are the troublemaker because you turned your back on God and worshipped Baal and other false gods."

183
A Contest on Mount Carmel
1 Kings 18

Elijah decided to prove to the people of Israel who their true God really was. He said to King Ahab, "Call all the people to Mount Carmel. Bring the 450 prophets of Baal with you and the 400 prophets of Asherah."

Then Elijah spoke to the people of Israel: "How long are you going to say you are God's people but worship Baal? If God is the true God, then worship him. But if Baal is really God, then follow him."

Then Elijah said, "I'm the only one of God's prophets left alive. Baal has 450 prophets. Let them take a bull for sacrifice and cut it up and put it on their altar, but don't light the fire. Then let them pray to Baal, and if he is really God, he will send fire to burn up the sacrifice."

The people all said, "That's a good idea."

So the 450 prophets began to pray to Baal, but nothing happened. They danced around; they even cut themselves with knives, but Baal didn't

answer them, because he was just an idol. Elijah made fun of them, "Maybe your god is asleep or taking a trip!" But still nothing happened.

184
Fire from Heaven

1 Kings 18

Then it was Elijah's turn. He gathered the people around him. He chose twelve large stones to represent the twelve tribes of Israel, and he repaired the broken-down altar of the Lord. Then he dug a ditch around it.

He killed a bull, cut it into pieces, and put the pieces on the altar. Three times he poured water over the altar so that it covered the sacrifice and filled the ditch around the altar.

Everything was ready. Elijah stood before the altar and prayed, "O Lord, you are a faithful God. Prove to these people that you are indeed the one true God so they will worship you again."

Instantly, fire swooped down from heaven and burned up the sacrifice, the wood, and the stones. It even dried up all the water in the ditch. The people all fell down on their faces and cried out, "Almighty God is the true God!"

Elijah told the people to grab the prophets of Baal. They took them to the Kishon Valley, and there Elijah killed all the false prophets.

185
God Sends Rain at Last

1 Kings 18

After Elijah had informed King Ahab that rain was on the way, he climbed to the top of Mount Carmel and knelt

down. He said to his servant, "Look out toward the sea; then tell me what you see."

The servant came back and said, "I don't see anything."

Elijah said, "Go again." He said this to his servant seven times.

Finally the servant returned and reported, "I see a very small cloud on the horizon. It's no larger than a man's hand."

"Good!" said Elijah. "Now go and tell Ahab that he'd better drive quickly down the mountain. Soon the rain will be so heavy he won't be able to make the trip."

Even as he spoke, the small cloud grew larger. In just moments the sky became black with storm clouds. The wind blew fiercely, and then the rain came. It poured! King Ahab was riding in his chariot to the city. God gave Elijah the strength to run faster than Ahab's chariot, and Elijah reached the city first!

186
An Angel Feeds Elijah

1 Kings 19

As soon as Ahab got home, he told Queen Jezebel everything that had happened on Mount Carmel. When he got to the part about how Elijah had killed all the prophets of Baal, she became terribly angry. She sent this message to Elijah: "By this time tomorrow, I will see to it that you are dead."

Elijah was afraid she would kill him, so he fled from the city. He travelled out into the desert, where, he hoped, Jezebel couldn't find him.

That night he told God, "You might as well take my life." Then he fell asleep.

An angel came and woke him. "Get up and eat," the angel said. Elijah was surprised to see some fresh bread and a jar of water on a rock nearby.

He ate and drank, then went back to sleep. Again the angel came. "Come and eat some more. You need strength for a long journey."

Again Elijah ate, and then he set out. He went to Mount Sinai, where he camped in a cave.

187
God Chooses a New Prophet

1 Kings 19

God asked Elijah what he was doing on Mount Sinai. Elijah said, "I've been trying to serve you well. I'm the only true believer left, and now your people want to kill me, too."

God answered, "Step outside the cave, Elijah, and stand before me as I pass by."

Elijah stood on the mountain, and a strong wind blew by, but that wasn't the Lord. Then an earthquake shook the land, but God wasn't in the earthquake. A fire came, but still God didn't pass by. Finally Elijah heard a small, quiet voice, and he knew God had come.

The voice said, "Elijah, why are you here?"

Again Elijah told God he was the only faithful believer left in Israel.

God replied, "Listen Elijah. You are not alone! There are seven thousand people who have never worshipped Baal. Now I want you to anoint a new king for Syria and one for Israel. Then find a man named Elisha. He will help you, and later he will take your place."

Elijah found Elisha ploughing in a field. Elijah threw his cloak around Elisha's shoulders. Elisha knew this meant he was to be Elijah's successor. He went home and celebrated with his family; then he joined Elijah and worked with him.

188
A Victory for Israel
1 Kings 20

King Ben-hadad of Aram planned to attack Samaria, the Israelite capital. He sent this message to King Ahab: "Give me your wives and children, silver and gold!" Ahab was afraid, so he agreed.

Then Ben-hadad sent another message: "My men will take whatever they want from your palace and your people's homes."

Ahab's advisors said, "Stand up to him!" So Ahab refused Ben-hadad's demand.

That made Ben-hadad angry. He sent this message to Ahab: "By tomorrow, Samaria will be just a pile of trash."

Ahab was feeling braver, so he replied, "Don't brag about it until you've done it!"

The Aramean army prepared to attack. Meanwhile, a prophet told Ahab, "The Lord will help you win. Then you will know he is the true God. Take part of your army and go out to meet the Arameans."

The battle started. The Israelites killed a great many Arameans. The rest panicked and ran away.

The next spring the Arameans attacked again, but again they were defeated. Ahab agreed not to kill Ben-hadad.

The prophet told Ahab that God would punish him because he had not killed Ben-hadad the way God had told him to.

189
Ahab and Jezebel's Sin
1 Kings 21

Naboth owned a vineyard near King Ahab's palace. Ahab wanted that vineyard for himself, so he offered to buy it. Naboth said, "It has been in my family for generations. I will never sell it."

Ahab was so disappointed that he went back to the palace and went to bed to sulk. Jezebel asked, "What is the matter with you?"

When Ahab told her, she was disgusted. "Are you the king or aren't you? You can have anything you want. I'll get Naboth's vineyard for you!"

She hired some men to say that they had heard Naboth saying bad things about God and about the king. Naboth was dragged outside the city walls, and the people stoned him to death.

When Jezebel heard he was dead, she said to Ahab, "Now you can have Naboth's vineyard."

But Elijah came to Ahab and scolded him for causing Naboth's death and stealing his property. "Now you, too, will die."

190

Ahab Dies in Battle

1 Kings 22

There was peace between Israel and Syria for three years, but the Syrians still held an Israelite city, and Ahab wanted it back. He asked Jehoshaphat, king of Judah, to help him recapture Ramoth-gilead.

Jehoshaphat said, "I'm willing, but let's ask for God's advice."

So Ahab asked four hundred of his heathen prophets if he should go to war. They all said, "Yes, God will let you win."

Jehoshaphat didn't trust them, and he asked, "Isn't there a real prophet of the Lord here?"

Ahab said, "Well, there's Micaiah, but I don't like him. He always

prophesies bad things about me."

But they asked Micaiah anyway, who said, "Go on to war."

Ahab said, "Tell me the truth."

Then Micaiah said, "I can see Israel's soldiers scattered like sheep without a shepherd."

Ahab knew the vision meant he would be killed. He said to Jehoshaphat, "See, he always says bad things about me!"

Then he threw Micaiah into prison. Ahab and Jehoshaphat went out to the battle. During the fighting, a stray arrow hit Ahab. He bled to death in his chariot.

191
The King's Men Chase Elijah

2 Kings 1

Ahab's son Ahaziah became the next king of Israel. He worshipped Baal and made God very angry. When he was hurt in a bad fall in the palace, he sent a messenger to ask an idol whether he would get well.

When Elijah heard this, he said to Ahaziah's messenger, "Why ask advice of an idol? Isn't there a real God you could ask? Tell Ahaziah he will die!"

The messenger delivered the message; then Ahaziah sent an army captain with fifty men to capture Elijah. The captain said, "Man of God, come with me."

Elijah answered, "If I am a man of God, fire will come from heaven and destroy you and your men!" Instantly fire fell on them and killed them.

Then the king sent another captain and fifty more men. This captain said,

"Man of God, you must come with me." Elijah answered him in the same way, and fire from God destroyed that group too.

Ahaziah tried once more. This captain knelt and begged Elijah for mercy. "Please don't destroy us." God told Elijah to go with the soldiers.

He went to Ahaziah and said, "You will die because you asked advice of a false god instead of the true God." Ahaziah did die, and his brother Joram became the new king.

192
A Heavenly Chariot Ride

2 Kings 2

God planned that Elijah should not die but be taken to heaven in a fiery chariot. Prophets at Jericho said, "Elisha, did you know that God is going to take Elijah away?" And Elisha said, "Of course I know."

Elisha and Elijah went to the Jordan River. Elijah rolled up his cloak and hit the water with it. The water parted, and they walked across on dry land. Elijah asked Elisha, "Before I go, what do you want me to do for you?"

Elisha asked for twice as much power as Elijah had. Elijah said, "If you see me when I go, you shall have it."

As they were talking, a chariot of fire came from heaven, and Elijah rode up to heaven. Elisha cried out, "I see the chariot and the horsemen of Israel!" Then he struck the water with Elijah's cloak. Again it opened up, and he walked across on dry land.

193
Elisha Does Miracles

2 Kings 2

Some prophets who had been waiting for Elisha said, "We can see that the spirit of Elijah now rests upon you! Shouldn't we go and look for Elijah?" Elisha said, "No, don't look for him."

The prophets kept insisting, so Elisha said, "You can look for him, but you won't find him."

Some men came to see Elisha and said, "We are from Jericho. The drinking water there makes us sick, and it keeps the land from producing good crops."

Elisha answered, "Bring me a bowl of salt."

They handed it to him, and he threw the salt into the village spring and said, "The Lord says he will heal the water. Now the land will produce abundantly again."

As Elisha walked back through Bethel, some young fellows began to laugh at him and call him names. He turned and shouted a curse at them in the name of the Lord. Just then two bears came out of the woods and attacked the young men, seriously injuring forty-two of them.

194
The Lord
Provides Water

2 Kings 3

The people of Moab were supposed to provide Israel with lambs and wool each year. One year they refused to do it anymore. Joram, the king of Israel, was angry. He asked Jehoshaphat to help him fight against Moab. Some Edomite soldiers helped too. After they had marched for several days, their water was gone, and they couldn't find any wells. A soldier suggested that they ask Elisha for advice. Elisha said, "Go out and dig many ditches, and the Lord will send plenty of water to fill them. And he will give you victory over Moab."

The men dug ditches, and water flowed across the land and filled them.

When the soldiers of Moab saw the water on the ground, the morning sun made it look like blood. They thought the enemy soldiers had been killing each other. They said, "Now we'll march in and finish them off and steal everything we want."

But the armies of Israel, Judah, and Edom completely defeated them and destroyed their land, just as Elisha had said.

195
The Wonderful Jar of Oil

2 Kings 4

The widow of a prophet came to tell Elisha, "My husband loved the Lord, as you know. But he died owing another man a lot of money. If I can't repay the debt, that man will take my boys away from me and make them his slaves. What can I do?"

Elisha said, "Don't you have something you can sell to raise the money?"

"All I have," she replied, "is a jar with some oil in it."

Elisha said, "Go to all your neighbours and friends and borrow every jar and bottle they can spare."

She took the jars and bottles to her home and closed the door. She poured oil from her jar into the first borrowed jar and filled it up. Then she filled another one and another – until the borrowed bottles and jars were all filled up.

At that very moment, the oil stopped appearing in her original jar.

She sold all the oil to a merchant and used the money to pay her husband's debt. She had enough money left to support herself and her sons.

196
A Special Room for Elisha

2 Kings 4

Elisha often stopped for dinner at the home of a rich woman in the town of Shunem. The rich woman said to her husband, "That prophet is really a man of God. Let's build a small guest room for him on the roof of our house, where he can stay when he is in Shunem."

One day Elisha and his servant, Gehazi, were in his rooftop room. Elisha sent Gehazi to bring the woman to his room.

Gehazi spoke to her on Elisha's behalf. "You have done so many kind things for me. I want to do something for you in return. Shall I ask the king or the general of the army for some favour for you?"

"No, thank you," she replied. "I don't need a thing."

After she had left, Elisha asked his servant, "Can you think of anything we could do for her?"

Gehazi said, "Well, she has no children. She will have no one to take care of her when she is old."

"Ask her to come back," said Elisha.

When she came to his doorway, Elisha said, "I promise that by this time next year, you will have a son."

She could hardly believe him, but the next year she and her husband had a baby boy.

197

A Dead Boy Lives Again

2 Kings 4

The woman of Shunem was very happy to have a little son, but one day he began to feel sick. His mother held him in her arms, but soon he died. She took him to Elisha's room and laid him on the bed. Then she went to find the prophet.

She found Elisha at Mount Carmel. She knelt at his feet and cried out, "Was it my idea that God give me a baby? You raised my hopes for nothing!" When she said that, Elisha realized that the boy was dead. He sent Gehazi to run on ahead and put Elisha's walking stick on the boy's face. But that didn't do any good.

When Elisha got there, he prayed that God would bring the child to life. Then he lay down on top of the body, and the flesh began to get warmer. Elisha got up and prayed, then lay down again. Suddenly the child sneezed several times – and came back to life! What joy there was in that home when Elisha gave the mother back her little boy – alive again!

198
The Poisonous Food

2 Kings 4

Elisha travelled to Gilgal, where a famine was causing much suffering. He taught classes of young prophets, and one day they got hungry. Elisha told the servants to prepare some stew. They went out into the fields to find vegetables, and one of them found some wild gourds on a vine.

No one knew whether those gourds were good to eat. They were so hungry that they put them in the stew.

When the prophets began to eat, one of them shouted, "Stop! I think something in this stew is poisonous!"

Elisha stirred a handful of flour into the pot. "Now you can eat it. It's perfectly safe." And it was.

A few days later Elisha did another miracle. Someone had given some corn and small loaves of barley bread. Elisha told Gehazi to serve it to the prophets.

Gehazi said, "But this little bit of food isn't enough to feed a hundred hungry men."

Elisha said, "God will provide enough for everyone, and there'll be some left over!"

When all the prophets had eaten, there was extra food left over, just as Elisha had said.

199
A Servant Girl's Advice

2 Kings 5

During a war between Aram and Israel, the Aramean army took some prisoners to be their slaves. One of them was a little girl, who became the maid of the wife of Naaman, the commander of the Aramean army.

Naaman and his wife were kind to the girl, and the girl felt sorry for Naaman because he had leprosy.

The girl said, "I know a prophet back in Samaria who could cure Naaman's leprosy."

Naaman told the king, and the king sent him to Samaria with a letter of introduction to the Israelite king. Naaman also took gifts of money and clothing.

The king read the letter and was very upset. "What can I do about this man's leprosy? The king of Aram is just trying to start another war with us."

Elisha heard about it and offered to help Naaman. Naaman went to Elisha's home, and Elisha sent out a message, telling him to go to the Jordan River and wash himself seven times.

Naaman was insulted. "We have better rivers in Aram than they have in Israel. Why didn't the prophet come out to me and call on his God? I'm going home!"

200
Naaman is Healed

2 Kings 5

Naaman's servants said, "Oh, sir, don't give up. If the prophet had told you to do something hard, you would have done it. Well, he's told you to do something very easy, so why not try this simple cure?"

So Naaman washed himself in the Jordan River seven times. When he came out the seventh time, the disease was gone!

Naaman was excited and happy. He and his men went back to Elisha's house, and Naaman apologized. He said, "Now I realize that the God of Israel is the one true God. Please take these gifts of gold and silver and the clothing I have brought."

Elisha said, "No. I would never accept payment for what I did. God would not want me to do that." Naaman kept urging him, but Elisha still refused the gifts.

Naaman said, "All right. But I want to take some of the dirt from the

ground because when I get home I will always make sacrifices on an altar to the true God. I'll never worship false gods again."

He said goodbye and started back to Aram, thankful to be healed.

201

A Greedy Servant

2 Kings 5

Gehazi had heard his master refuse Naaman's gifts. After Naaman left, Gehazi thought, "What a waste! I think I'll go and get some for myself!"

Gehazi caught up with Naaman. Naaman asked, "Is something the matter?"

Gehazi answered, "No, but Elisha has two visitors, and he would like to have a bar of silver and two of the sets of clothing to give them."

Naaman believed Gehazi's lie and said, "Of course. I will give you twice as much as you asked for." And he told his servants to put the silver and clothes in bags and carry them home for Gehazi.

When they got there, Gehazi took the bags from the servants and hid them in his own house. Then he went back to Elisha, who asked, "Where have you been, Gehazi?"

"I didn't go anywhere," Gehazi said.

"Listen, because of your greed and your lies and trickery, you and all your descendants are going to have leprosy instead of Naaman."

Immediately Gehazi's skin became white with the terrible disease of leprosy.

202
The Axe That Floated and the Blind Army

2 Kings 6

The school of the prophets was growing, and their building wasn't large enough. They said to Elisha, "Let's build a new school building." Elisha agreed, so they went to the riverbank to cut logs. One of the students had borrowed an axe. He was very upset when the iron head of his axe became loose, fell into the river, and sank.

Elisha threw a stick into the water. The axe head floated to the surface, and the young man got it back.

When Aram was at war with Israel, the king of Aram gave some battle plans to one of his generals. Elisha warned the king of Israel about the plans. The Aramean king thought there must be a spy in his troops. But one of his soldiers said, "No, it's that prophet Elisha. God reveals secrets to him."

"Then we'll kill him," the king said. He sent soldiers to capture Elisha, but God protected Elisha by blinding all the soldiers. Elisha led them into Israel's capital city and then let them see again! The Israelite king wanted to kill them, but Elisha said no. Instead they fed the soldiers and let them go home.

203
A Terrible Food Shortage

2 Kings 6–7

King Ben-hadad attacked Samaria. His army surrounded the city and kept any food from being brought in. The people in Samaria became extremely hungry. Some even killed and ate other people.

King Joram decided it was all Elisha's fault. He said, "When I find him, I'm going to kill him." Joram wouldn't admit that the real cause of the fighting and the hunger was his own wickedness. He had forgotten Israel's true God and worshipped idols.

But he was sad to see his people suffering. He wore a rough garment next to his skin to remind himself of their needs.

Elisha heard about the king's threats, so he stayed inside his house. He said to his friends, "Guard the door. Keep the king's messenger outside. Soon the king will come after me himself."

When Joram came, Elisha told him that God had promised to end the food shortage the next day. "Food will be so plentiful," he said, "that you'll be able to buy flour and grain for a very low price."

204
Four Lepers Share with Others

2 Kings 7

Four lepers lived just outside the gate of Samaria. They were starving and said, "Let's go over to the Aramean camp and surrender. If they don't kill us, they might give us a little food."

When the lepers arrived, not a single soldier was there. God had made the Arameans think they were under attack. So they had run away, leaving everything in their camp!

The lepers found a lot of food in one tent, and they ate all they wanted. Then they found clothing and gold and silver.

They grabbed everything they could carry and hid it. Then they started back for more.

Suddenly they said, "We shouldn't be taking all this stuff for ourselves. We should share it with the suffering people in the city."

The lepers hurried back to the gate of Samaria and called to the guards. "We've found a lot of food in the Aramean camp. The soldiers have left; we can take all we want."

When they were sure it wasn't a trap, the people of the city rushed over to the camp and helped themselves.

205

A Woman Gets Her Land Back

2 Kings 8

The woman whose little boy Elisha brought back to life took Elisha's advice and left Israel until the famine was over. One day, after the famine had ended, Gehazi, Elisha's servant, was talking to the king.

The king said, "I want to know more about Elisha. Tell me some of the wonderful miracles he has done."

The servant told him about the woman with the little boy. Just then, she and her son walked into the palace. She had come to see the king about getting her land and home back.

Gehazi said, "This is the woman I was telling you about, Your Majesty. And this is the boy who was dead."

The king asked her, "Did all those things really happen to you?"

"Yes," she said. "That's exactly what happened."

So the king arranged for her to get back her house and land. He even gave her money to pay for the crops that had been harvested from her land during the seven years she had been gone.

206

Hazael Commits Murder

2 Kings 8

While Elisha was in Damascus, King Ben-hadad got sick. Ben-hadad sent a messenger named Hazael to Elisha. "Ask him to find out from God whether I will ever get well."

Hazael found Elisha and asked him, "Will my king recover from this illness?"

Elisha replied, "Tell him I said he will get well. It's not really true because God has told me that he will die." He started to cry.

"Why are you crying, sir?" Hazael asked.

"Because I know you are going to make my people suffer. You are going to burn down buildings. You will kill men and little children and mothers who are expecting babies."

Hazael was horrified. "Do you think I'm some kind of animal, that I would do such things?" he asked.

Elisha replied, "God has revealed to me that you will be the king of Aram."

When Hazael went back to the king, he told him that Elisha had said he would get well. Then Hazael held a wet blanket over the king's face. Ben-hadad couldn't breathe, so he died, and Hazael became the king in his place.

207
Jehu Will Be King

2 Kings 9

Elisha gave one of the student prophets a little bottle of oil and told him to go and find Jehu, the son of Jehoshaphat. Elisha said, "Speak with him privately. Tell him that he is to be king, and pour the oil over his head to anoint him. Then get out of there quickly."

The prophet found Jehu with a group of other army officers. "Sir," he said, "I wish to speak to you alone."

Jehu followed him out to a private place, and there the prophet poured the oil over Jehu's head. "Sir, you are to be the next king," the prophet said. "The Lord God wants you to destroy Ahab's household and avenge the death of God's prophets. Jezebel shall die a violent death, and dogs will eat her body."

When the prophet had gone, Jehu went back to his friends. They asked him who that strange man was and what he had wanted.

Jehu told them what the prophet had said about his becoming king. His friends were glad to hear the news. They shouted, "Jehu is the king! Long live the king!"

208
A Wicked Queen Dies

2 Kings 9

Jehu wanted to get to Jezreel before anyone could tell King Joram that there was going to be a new king. He got into his chariot and rode very fast to Jezreel. King Joram got into his chariot with King Ahaziah of Judah, who was visiting him, and rode out to meet Jehu.

Joram asked, "Are you coming as a friend?"

Jehu answered, "How can we be friends when you do so many evil things, just like your mother, Jezebel?"

Joram was afraid and tried to escape, but Jehu killed him and King Ahaziah too.

Jezebel waited for Jehu at an upstairs window. When he arrived, she shouted, "You murderer!"

Jehu called out, "Is anyone up there on my side? If so, throw her down!"

Several men pushed Jezebel out of the window, and the fall killed her. Her body was eaten by dogs. That is just what Elisha had said would happen to that wicked, idol-worshipping queen.

209
The Death of a Powerful Prophet

2 Kings 10; 13

King Jehu destroyed Ahab's family. Jehu was not a good king. Years later his grandson, Jehoash, became king. Elisha got sick. He knew he was going to die. King Jehoash visited him, and Elisha said, "Put an arrow into your bow." Jehoash did, and Elisha put his hands over the king's hands. Together they pulled back the bowstring and shot the arrow through an open window.

Elisha said, "This is a sign that Israel is going to be free of the Arameans."

Then the prophet told the king to hit the floor with a bundle of arrows. The king struck the floor three times, then stopped.

Elisha said, "You stopped too soon. Now you will only defeat Aram three times. If you had kept going, you would have kept on defeating the Arameans until they were destroyed."

Elisha died and was buried. One day some men were taking a body to be

buried. They saw some robbers coming, so they put the dead man in Elisha's tomb and ran away. As soon as the dead body touched Elisha's bones, the man came back to life again.

Even in death, Elisha could do miracles!

—————— 210 ——————
God's Prophets Warn Israel

2 Kings 14; Amos; Hosea

Israel fought and defeated Aram three times. After Jehoash died, his son, Jeroboam II, became king. He, too, was an idol-worshipping king. God now chose new prophets. One of these was Amos, a shepherd. God gave Amos harsh words of warning for the people of Israel.

God said, "The cities of Israel have sinned again and again, and I will not forget it. Now, prepare yourselves for the punishment I will send."

To be sure they understood, God said, "A carpenter uses a plumb line to check how straight a wall is. I have checked you against my plumb line, and you are crooked with sin!"

Then he said they were like ripe fruit, ready to be picked. That meant they were ready to receive his punishment. Hosea scolded the people, too, saying, "You are like a wife who isn't loving and faithful to her husband. You have left God and loved idols instead." Hosea said they were like people who chased the wind. In worshipping idols they were running after something they couldn't even touch because the false gods weren't real.

211
The Death of a Nation

2 Kings 15–17

Jeroboam II was followed by several other kings, all of them idol-worshippers. Not one of the kings of Israel was faithful to God. They all led the people away from true worship.

God had promised Israel that he would bless them and protect them if they were faithful to him. But for more than two hundred years they had been unfaithful, so God took away his protection.

The king of Assyria attacked Israel and forced King Hoshea to pay taxes to Assyria. After a while Hoshea secretly asked the king of Egypt to help free him from Assyria's rule, and he stopped paying the tax money.

The Assyrian king, Shalmaneser, heard about Hoshea's deal with Egypt, and it made him angry.

Shalmaneser grabbed Hoshea and put him in prison. For three years his large army attacked Samaria, the capital of Israel.

Finally the city surrendered. The citizens of Israel became prisoners of war and were shipped off to live in Assyria.

Then Shalmaneser filled up Samaria with people from foreign cities. They were all idol-worshippers and cared nothing about God. What a sad thing to happen in the land God had prepared for his own people!

212
Meanwhile, Back in Judah…

1 Kings 14–15; 2 Chronicles 15–16

After King Solomon died, his kingdom was divided into two groups of tribes. Israel was the larger group, and Judah the smaller. It was bad enough being divided into two kingdoms, but it was even worse when the two kingdoms fought against each other.

During one of those fights, the king of Judah scolded Israel for not having a king from King David's family. He said, "You have a much bigger army than we do, but because you worship the gold calf idols your king made for you, the Lord our God will help us defeat you." And that's just what happened.

One of the kings of Judah was Asa. As long as he trusted God, he could defeat his enemies. But when Asa hired the Aramean army to defend him instead of asking for God's help, God wasn't pleased and sent a prophet to scold him.

The prophet said, "You should have trusted the Lord. From now on, he will let your enemies defeat you."

Asa was disgusted with the prophet and threw him in jail. Then the king became ill and died. Jehoshaphat became the next king of Judah.

213
A Faithful King

1 Kings 22; 2 Chronicles 17–20

King Jehoshaphat of Judah tried to please God all of his life, and his people respected and loved him. He chose teachers of the Law and sent them out to teach the people how to obey God. Even heathen people liked Jehoshaphat, and they sent him gifts of money and animals. Not since Solomon had there been such a popular and rich king.

Jehoshaphat's son married the daughter of King Ahab. Because of the marriage, Jehoshaphat went to Israel to visit Ahab. He was there to help when Ahab was at war with Aram. This didn't please God.

Jehoshaphat appointed honest judges to punish criminals and protect the innocent. He told the judges, "You must see that justice is done. You are responsible to God. He sees everything you do."

Jehoshaphat went into partnership with one of the wicked Israelite kings. They formed a shipping company.

A prophet said to Jehoshaphat, "God doesn't want you to have this business arrangement with an ungodly king. The Lord is going to destroy your business."

Soon a storm at sea wrecked all the ships, and that was the end of the partnership.

214

God Gives Judah a Victory

2 Chronicles 20

Judah was a small country with a small army, so Jehoshaphat was worried when he heard that the armies of Moab, Ammon, and Edom were joining to attack them. He asked for God's help, then told everyone to fast and pray. Many of the people of Judah came to Jerusalem and stood around the Temple while they prayed.

God's Spirit filled a man named Jahaziel, who gave them a message from God: "Don't worry. The battle is not yours but God's. You won't even have to fight. Go prepared to attack; then see how God helps you."

The next morning Jehoshaphat led his army out. While Jehoshaphat's choir sang songs of praise, the enemy troops started to fight among themselves. By the time Judah's army arrived, the ground was covered with dead bodies. Judah's army had defeated the enemies without a fight.

They returned home, singing and shouting for joy. An orchestra played as they marched into Jerusalem, praising God for the great victory he had given them.

215

The King's Illness and Death

2 Chronicles 21

Before Jehoshaphat died, he made a will, dividing up his money and possessions among his sons. He decided that Jehoram, his oldest son, should be the next king of Judah. Unfortunately Jehoram had married Athaliah, Ahab and Jezebel's daughter.

Like her parents, Athaliah was an idol-worshipper, and she led Jehoram away from God. When Jehoram became king, he put up idols for the people of Judah to worship, and soon many of them were unfaithful to the Lord.

Jehoram was afraid his six brothers would try to take the kingdom away from him, so he murdered them. God was displeased with him. When Jehoram went to war, God did not help him, and he lost his control over the Edomites.

Elijah sent him a letter with a message from God. It said, "You are not like your father, Jehoshaphat. You are a murderer and an idol-worshipper, and you have led my people away from me. I am going to send you a terrible sickness, and after you have suffered much pain, you will die."

Before Jehoram died, God sent some enemy troops to attack Judah. They looted the palace and captured the king's wives and most of his sons. Only his youngest son, Ahaziah, was left.

216

A Baby Prince is Hidden

2 Chronicles 22–23

Ahaziah was the only royal son left to become king, but his mother, Athaliah, had taught him to worship idols, and he cared nothing for God. He ruled for only a year because he happened to be visiting in Israel when Jehu assassinated Israel's king and took over the throne. Ahaziah got caught in that rebellion and was also killed.

Athaliah saw her chance to become the ruler of Judah, so she killed Ahaziah's sons, her own grandsons, in order to make herself queen. But Joash, her one-year-old grandson had disappeared. Ahaziah's sister was married to the priest Jehoiada, and they had hidden the baby in the Temple to protect him.

Wicked Queen Athaliah ruled Judah for six years until finally Jehoiada decided to reveal his secret to the Levite ministers in the Temple, and they worked out a plan. The priests and leaders from all over Judah gathered at the Temple. Then Jehoiada brought Joash out of his hiding place. He poured oil over the boy's head and crowned him king. The people in the Temple shouted, "Long live the king!"

217

Joash, a Wise Young King

2 Chronicles 23–24

When Joash was crowned king the trumpeters blew their horns, choirs sang, an orchestra played, and all the people joined in singing a hymn of praise! Soon Athaliah heard the noise and came to see what was going on. She was shocked to see Joash standing

there as the new king. In great anger she screamed, "This is treason!" Jehoiada said to the soldiers, "Take her out to the stable and kill her, and get rid of anyone who tries to help her." Then Jehoiada made a promise before God that he and Joash and all the people would love and worship only the true God. Everyone rushed out and started destroying idols and heathen altars. They tore down the temple of Baal and killed its priest. The high priest put the Levites in charge of worship in the Temple, just as the Lord had instructed King David.

The priests, nobles, and all the people took Joash from the Temple and seated him on the throne in the palace. And the country was peaceful at last.

Joash grew up loving God and wanting to please him. Jehoiada continued to give him good advice after he became king. When Joash was old enough to be married, Jehoiada chose good wives for him, and he had several children.

218

Joash Repairs the Temple

2 Chronicles 24

While Judah was ruled by idol-worshippers, the Temple fell into disrepair. Some of Queen Athaliah's sons had broken in and stolen items of worship and had taken them to the Baal temple.

King Joash was upset to see God's house so neglected. He asked Jehoiada, "Shouldn't we be collecting the Temple tax and taking better care of the Temple?"

King Joash put a chest at the gate of the Temple for people to put their money in. Then he sent word all over the country that everyone should pay the Temple tax that Moses had established many years before. The officials of the land and all the other people were happy to do this, and soon the chest was full of money.

The priests emptied it again and again, but the chest kept being filled with the people's taxes and gifts. Soon there was enough to pay for the repairs.

Craftsmen worked hard to bring the Temple back to its original beauty and usefulness. Some of the money was used to manufacture replacement items that had been stolen.

As long as Jehoiada lived, Joash and the people worshipped God faithfully.

— 219 —
The Death of Joash
2 Chronicles 24

After Jehoiada died, the king and many of his people stopped going to the Temple for worship. God was angry with them and sent prophets to warn them, but they wouldn't listen.

Jehoiada's son, Zechariah, called everyone together and said, "God wants to know why you are turning away from him and disobeying his commandments. If you desert God, he will not help you when you need him."

Jehoiada had taken care of Joash when he was a baby and had protected him from his wicked grandmother, Athaliah. He had made him king of Judah and had taught him to love and worship God. In spite of all that, Joash murdered Jehoiada's son, Zechariah. As Zechariah died, he said, "May God make you pay for what you are doing." Later the Arameans brought an army against Judah. As Zechariah had predicted, God didn't help Judah. The Aramean army won the battle and left Joash badly wounded. Some of Joash's men despised him for killing Zechariah, and so they killed him as he lay in his bed.

— 220 —
A New King for Judah
2 Chronicles 25

Joash's son Amaziah became the next king. The first thing he did was to execute the men who had killed his father. Most of the time King Amaziah did good things, but his heart wasn't in it. He brought together a large army – 300,000 soldiers from Judah and another 100,000 from Israel to help him fight the Edomites.

A prophet came to Amaziah and said, "Your Majesty, you must not hire soldiers from Israel to fight in your army because the Lord isn't blessing them. If you use them, God will let you be defeated in battle."

Amaziah replied, "I've already paid them a lot of money. I'll lose that if I send them home."

The prophet said, "Obeying God is more important than the 100 talents of silver you spent."

So Amaziah sent the soldiers back home. They were angry with him for changing his mind. Then he took his own soldiers to fight the Edomites, and God helped him win a great victory. But in spite of God's help, Amaziah decided to bring back many of the Edomites' idols and set them up to be worshipped in Judah.

221
King Uzziah Becomes a Leper

2 Chronicles 25–26

The Lord was angry with Amaziah for bringing idols to Judah, so again God sent the prophet to scold Amaziah. "Did these false gods help you fight Edom?"

"Mind your own business, or I'll kill you!" Amaziah roared.

The prophet answered bravely, "God is going to destroy you because you worship idols and don't listen to my warnings."

Amaziah foolishly declared war on Israel. His army was badly defeated, and he was taken prisoner. Amaziah's own people were angry with him for getting them into trouble. They killed him as he was trying to escape, so his son Uzziah became king.

Uzziah was only sixteen years old. He wanted to be a good king, and he had a wise counsellor named Zechariah. God helped Uzziah build Judah into a powerful nation with a strong army.

Later Uzziah's success and power began to change him. One day he entered the Most Holy Place in the Temple, where only priests were allowed to go, and burned incense at the altar. The high priest and other priests told him to get out or the Lord would punish him. Uzziah refused to leave. Soon the skin on his forehead became white and lumpy with leprosy. He remained a leper for the rest of his life, and his son Jotham became king.

222
Isaiah Says a Saviour Will Come

2 Chronicles 27; Isaiah

Jotham was twenty-five when he was crowned king. He obeyed God and tried to lead the people in the right way. Like his father, he successfully fought against the Ammonites and forced them to pay a lot of money each year, plus 50,000 sacks of wheat and 50,000 sacks of barley.

Even though Jotham obeyed the Lord, most of his people were being disobedient. God sent one of his greatest prophets, Isaiah, to advise them and warn them about their sins.

Through Isaiah, God told them that if they obeyed him he would bless them, but if they worshipped idols, he would leave them and they would have much trouble and sorrow. He warned them that if they carried on disobeying him, enemy tribes would capture them and seize their Promised Land.

Some of Isaiah's prophecy was about Jesus, God's Son, who would become the Saviour of the world. Seven hundred years later these words came true. Isaiah knew what would happen in the future because he was God's prophet and God revealed the future to him.

223
King Ahaz Nails the Temple Shut

2 Chronicles 28

Jotham died after ruling Judah for sixteen years. He had been faithful to God, but his son Ahaz wasn't like him. When Ahaz became king, he worshipped the false god Baal. But even worse than that, he offered his own children on a heathen altar.

To punish him, God let the Aramean and Israelite armies defeat him in war. Many of his people were taken captive to Aram, and the army of Israel killed thousands of Judah's soldiers, including the king's son.

The Israelites also took away 200,000 women and children from Judah. A prophet rebuked them, saying, "God wants to use you to punish Judah, but you are going too far." Then they let some of the captives go.

Ahaz needed help against his enemies, so he hired troops from King Tiglath-pileser of Assyria. The king helped him defeat Aram and capture Damascus, but then he turned against Ahaz.

Ahaz destroyed some of the beautiful things in the Temple. Finally he nailed the Temple doors shut.

Everywhere the people looked, they saw idols that their king had put up. And God was disappointed in Judah and angry with King Ahaz.

224
Hezekiah Opens God's House

2 Chronicles 29

Though Ahaz had been a bad king, his son Hezekiah loved God. Hezekiah was king of Judah for twenty-nine years, and he brought the country back to the Lord. In the very first month he was king, Hezekiah opened up the Temple. He called in the Levites and priests and said to them, "Purify yourselves according to the Law, and then clean up God's house of worship."

It took them sixteen days to prepare the Temple for worship. Then they reported to Hezekiah, "Everything is clean and ready for use."

The next day Hezekiah went to the Temple with the leaders of the city. He took many animals for sacrifice. The priests made burnt offerings and sin offerings for all of the people. The king appointed some Levites to be in an orchestra and others to play trumpets, just as it had been done in King David's time. Then they all joined in the worship of God. How happy King Hezekiah and all his people were to be obeying God once again in his holy Temple!

— 225 —
Passover: A Happy Time Again
2 Chronicles 30

For many years the people in Judah had not celebrated the Passover feast that reminded them of the time when God led them out of Egypt. Now Hezekiah was trying to obey all of God's commands, and he wanted the people to celebrate the Passover again. He invited everyone to come to Jerusalem and join in the celebration.

He wanted all the priests and Levites to get ready for it too. Usually the Passover was in April, but because there wasn't enough time to get ready that early, the king decided to have it in May.

What a great time they had! The festival lasted for seven days and was filled with praise and music and reading of God's Word. The people were so happy that they stayed for another week.

When they went back to their homes in different parts of the country, they tore down idols and heathen altars. They wanted their country to be a place where only the true God was worshipped.

226
An Angel Fights for Judah
2 Chronicles 32

The king of Assyria was planning to attack Jerusalem. Hezekiah encouraged his soldiers. "Don't be afraid! God will protect us." But Hezekiah was afraid of the Assyrians' army. He sent their king some gifts, hoping to get them to call off their attack.

They went away for a while, but later their king sent some soldiers to boast about what he was going to do. They called to the watchmen on the wall, "Don't believe what Hezekiah says about God's protection. You might as well surrender and be our slaves."

Hezekiah prayed and asked the prophet Isaiah to pray too. Isaiah sent the king this message: "Do not be afraid. God will punish the king of Assyria and send him home. There he will be killed."

The Assyrian king sent a threatening letter. Hezekiah took the letter to the Temple and had a prayer meeting. God sent him an answer through Isaiah: "I will do as you have asked. The Assyrian army will stay away from Jerusalem."

That night God sent his angel of death to the Assyrian camp, and thousands of soldiers died. Then the Assyrian king went home. But while he was worshipping his idol, some of his sons assassinated him.

227
Hezekiah's Life is Lengthened
2 Kings 20; 2 Chronicles 32

King Hezekiah fell ill. Isaiah said, "You must prepare yourself because God has said you are going to die."

Hezekiah turned his face toward the wall and cried, "Oh, Lord! Please remember me."

As Isaiah left, the Lord said to him, "Go back and tell Hezekiah that I have heard his prayer."

Isaiah hurried back and told Hezekiah, "The Lord is going to heal you! You will be well enough to worship at the Temple. And God will let you live another fifteen years."

Hezekiah said, "Give me a sign that the Lord will heal me."

Isaiah answered, "Shall the shadow move backwards or forwards?"

Hezekiah asked for the shadow to move back ten steps and the Lord performed this sign.

King Hezekiah became very rich and powerful, but he forgot to give God the credit. He acted as if he had done it all himself.

So Hezekiah used his extra fifteen years very unwisely. He was selfish and proud, and his people slipped back into idol worship. Isaiah and another prophet, Micah, tried to warn Hezekiah and the people, but they wouldn't listen.

228
King Manasseh's Heart is Changed

2 Chronicles 33

After Hezekiah died, his twelve-year-old son Manasseh became king. He turned the people of Judah back to the worship of idols. He even put up false gods in the Temple! Manasseh sacrificed his own children on altars, and he got advice from fortune-tellers and magicians instead of from God.

God's prophets warned him, but the king didn't listen. Finally the Lord let the Assyrian troops come and take Manasseh captive. They led him away to Babylon as their prisoner. There he had time to think about all his mistakes. Manasseh became really sorry for his foolishness and his sin. He cried out to God and asked for help. God knew that Manasseh was truly sorry, so God forgave him.

Manasseh's captors took him back to Jerusalem. The king tore down the idols he had built and repaired the city wall to protect Jerusalem. He also removed the false gods from the Temple and got it ready for the true worship of God.

— 229 —
Another Young King
2 Chronicles 34

Manasseh's son Amon ruled for two years; then he was assassinated. His eight-year-old son Josiah became the next king. Josiah loved God and wanted to please him. As Josiah grew up he wanted to learn as much as he could about the Lord.

Josiah finished tearing down the heathen altars and idols his grandfather Manasseh had built. Josiah even went around to neighbouring tribes and destroyed idols there. In his twenties Josiah began repairing parts of the Temple that had been neglected. His helpers, Shaphan, Maaseiah, and Joah, arranged for collecting boxes to be put at the Temple gates. These were guarded by some of the Levites.

The money given by the people was used to pay craftsmen and to buy materials. Some of the Levites played and sang music to entertain and encourage the workmen. Other Levites were put in charge of the workmen. It was a busy place, and all the people worked joyfully because they wanted God's house to be a beautiful place of worship.

— 230 —
Josiah Celebrates Passover
2 Chronicles 34–35

While Hilkiah, the high priest, was working in the Temple, he found an old scroll. It was a copy of the Law God had given to Moses. Hilkiah showed it to Shaphan, the king's assistant.

Shaphan took it to King Josiah and said, "Everything is going well at the Temple. The money is coming in, and the workmen are being paid. And look, Hilkiah found this old scroll. It is the Law of Moses. I'll read it to you."

As Josiah listened, he realized that his people had not always kept the rules. Josiah felt terrible and said to the priests, "No wonder we've had so much trouble. Go to the Temple and pray for our country and for Israel."

The priests talked to Huldah, one of God's prophets. She said, "God has been punishing his people for not obeying his Law. Tell the king how to make it right, and the Lord will forgive the nation."

Josiah did everything he could to make up for the sins of the nation. He arranged for the Passover to be celebrated again, and everyone turned out for the celebration.

Later, King Josiah was killed in a battle with the king of Egypt. His people were very sad.

231
Judah Ruled by Babylon

2 Chronicles 36; Jeremiah 21

Josiah's son Jehoahaz was a weak king. He was captured by the pharaoh of Egypt, who appointed Jehoahaz's brother Jehoiakim to take over. But soon a very powerful king named Nebuchadnezzar came from Babylon and took control of Judah. Nebuchadnezzar stole things from the Temple and put them in his heathen temple in Babylon.

Jehoiakim died after a few years. His son became king for a short time, but it wasn't long before Jehoiakim's brother Zedekiah took his place. Zedekiah ruled for about eleven years, but he didn't worship God, and he ignored Jeremiah's good advice. He had no real power of his own but let King Nebuchadnezzar control him.

Zedekiah had to pay a great deal of money to Nebuchadnezzar in taxes each year. Zedekiah wasn't very loyal or cooperative, so Nebuchadnezzar invaded Judah and attacked Jerusalem.

Zedekiah asked Jeremiah to pray for God's help. But it was too late. God sent this message through Jeremiah: "If you surrender and are obedient slaves, you will be all right. But if you are stubborn and rebellious, you will all die."

God told Jeremiah to wear a heavy wooden yoke on his shoulders, showing how the people should be Nebuchadnezzar's slaves.

232

Jeremiah is Put into a Well

Jeremiah 27; 38

As Jeremiah walked around wearing
the yoke, the leaders of the city became
angry with him. They asked the king to
kill the prophet. "His gloomy messages
are bad for morale. He sounds like a
traitor."

The king said they could punish
Jeremiah, so they let him down into a
deep, dark, muddy well.

One of the king's men told him what
the leaders had done to Jeremiah. "He
will starve down there, and he is the
Lord's prophet. What they have done is
cruel."

The king sent some men to get
Jeremiah out of the well. They hauled
him up to the surface. They didn't let
him go but kept him in the prison.

233

Ezekiel Teaches Object Lessons

Ezekiel 1; 4–5

Ezekiel, a priest, was among the people
of Judah taken away to Babylon by
Nebuchadnezzar. God talked to people
through his special messengers called
prophets. Sometimes he talked to the
prophets through dreams or visions.
One day Ezekiel had a vision of God's
throne and all the glory of heaven, and
it made him bow and worship God.

Then God said, "I want you to warn
all the captives by using object lessons.
Draw a picture of Jerusalem on a piece
of clay, and put a wall in front of it.

Then build a fort outside the wall. Next,
you must lie down in front of it and
pretend to be starving. The people will
know it is because of Nebuchadnezzar's
attack on Jerusalem."

For the next object lesson, Ezekiel
cut off his hair and beard and divided
it into three parts. He burned one part,
cut up one part, and blew away the third
part. This showed that some people
would starve when the city was burned
up, some would be killed outside the
city, and some would be scattered
elsewhere.

234
No One Believes Ezekiel

Ezekiel 8–11

Ezekiel had another vision. He seemed to be picked up by the hair and whisked away to Jerusalem. The Lord showed him the idols his people had been worshipping, then told him to look in an inner room of the Temple.

There he saw leaders of Judah bowing down to pictures of false gods and other people worshipping the sun.

The Lord told Ezekiel he was going to punish his people by destroying their city, and that if they cried out to him he wouldn't listen or help them.

Then Ezekiel found himself being taken through the sky, back to Babylon. Ezekiel told the other captured Jews what he had seen, but they chose not to believe him. They preferred to believe the lies of the false prophets – that the people of Jerusalem would not be punished for their sins and that Nebuchadnezzar would never burn the city and the Temple.

235
God's Special Messenger

Ezekiel 12

Ezekiel wrote down everything God told him, then acted it out to the people. For the next object lesson he made a hole in the back wall of his house at night and pretended he was moving out. He took some of his belongings with him. "This is like a play on a stage," he told them. "King Zedekiah will try to get away from Jerusalem, but he will be caught and brought back here as a prisoner."

Then Ezekiel acted as if he was badly frightened. This showed how scared the people of Jerusalem would be when the attack came. God even revealed to Ezekiel what day these things would happen.

When Jerusalem was conquered three years later, Ezekiel's fellow captives realized he had been telling the truth.

236
God Sends Good News

Ezekiel 37

God still loved Israel and Judah. He gave Ezekiel more messages to encourage the people and give them a promise for the future. First God gave Ezekiel a vision of a big field covered with human skeletons. God told Ezekiel to say to the bones, "Listen to what God is going to do. He will put flesh on you and let you breathe and become alive!"

As Ezekiel watched, those words came true. Flesh grew on the bones, and the bones joined together and became human forms. Then Ezekiel called to the wind to blow on the bodies and put breath into them. Immediately the bodies came to life and were like a huge army.

God said to Ezekiel, "This shows what is going to happen to Israel and Judah. They will receive new life and strength and will become powerful again."

God told Ezekiel to pick up two

sticks and name one of them Israel and the other one Judah. As Ezekiel held the sticks in his hand, they became one stick. This showed that the two countries would join together again, as in the days of David and Solomon.

237

The Beautiful City is Burned

2 Chronicles 36; Jeremiah 52

Back in Jerusalem, King Zedekiah sent for Jeremiah. "I want you to tell me the truth about what is going to happen," the king said.

Jeremiah answered, "If I do, you will probably kill me!"

"I promise not to kill you," the king said.

Jeremiah said, "If you and your people surrender peaceably and become Nebuchadnezzar's slaves, you will be kept from harm, and the city will be saved."

Zedekiah was afraid to do that, so he held out against Nebuchadnezzar. The Babylonian army kept attacking Jerusalem. No supplies could get into the city, so the people were in danger of starvation.

Zedekiah tried to escape, but he was captured and taken to Nebuchadnezzar. As Zedekiah watched, Nebuchadnezzar killed Zedekiah's two sons and then blinded Zedekiah. He spent the rest of his life in a Babylonian prison.

The Babylonian army looted Jerusalem and burned down the beautiful Temple, the palaces, and the homes. They smashed the walls of the city and killed many of the people. The rest of the people became slaves in Babylon. The history of the kingdom of Judah came to a sad end because of the people's sin and indifference to God.

— 238 —
Judah – a Lonely, Deserted Country

2 Kings 25; Jeremiah 40–43

Nebuchadnezzar told his army general to be kind to Jeremiah. The general released Jeremiah and said, "You may go with me to Babylon, where you will be treated well, or you may stay here."

Jeremiah decided to stay, so the general gave him a supply of food and some money. Jeremiah stayed with Gedaliah, the governor Nebuchadnezzar had appointed.

A few of the people of Judah ran away when they knew Nebuchadnezzar was going to capture the city. But after the war, Gedaliah was left in charge, so the people of Judah asked if they could come back. Gedaliah said, "Yes. Obey the king of Babylon, and everything will go well for you."

After a while the Ammonites had Gedaliah killed, and the rest of the people were afraid Nebuchadnezzar would punish them because of Gedaliah's death. They asked Jeremiah what they should do.

The Lord sent them this answer: "Stay here in Judah and you will be safe."

But the people didn't believe the Lord. They ran away to Egypt and made Jeremiah go with them. So Judah was deserted and lying in ruins.

The people had insisted on their own way, so Judah and Israel were in captivity, and God's special people had lost their home in the Promised Land.

— 239 —
Daniel and His Friends

Daniel 1

Daniel lived in Jerusalem. He loved his parents, and he obeyed everything they taught him about worshipping God and following the Law. When Nebuchadnezzar destroyed Jerusalem, Daniel was one of the captives taken to Babylon. The king chose some of

the smartest and strongest boys from Judah to go to a special school where they would spend three years studying important subjects. Daniel was one of the boys chosen, along with three of his best friends – Shadrach, Meshach, and Abednego.

Nebuchadnezzar didn't care about God. He expected the boys to do wrong things sometimes. But when they were offered food and wine that had been used in idol worship, the boys asked to be excused from eating it.

Their teacher said, "If you become weak and sick, the king will punish me."

Daniel said, "Just give us plain vegetables and water for ten days. We'll be fine."

Daniel and his friends went on to become the wisest students of all. And God gave Daniel the special gift of understanding dreams.

240
The King Has a Scary Dream

Daniel 2

Nebuchadnezzar gave Daniel and his friends good jobs and made Daniel one of his special counsellors. One night the king had a frightening dream. When King Nebuchadnezzar awoke, he knew his dream had been scary, but he couldn't remember what it was about. This worried him. The king asked his magicians and astrologers to tell him what he had dreamed, but they couldn't.

They said, "Tell us what you dreamed, and we'll tell you what it means."

The king answered, "I told you – I can't remember. Tell me what I dreamed, and I will reward you. If you can't tell me, I'll kill you!"

His wise men still couldn't answer him, and this made the king furiously angry. They said, "What you ask is impossible. Nobody in the world can tell people what they dream."

The king ordered all his wise men to be brought before him. Daniel and his friends were in the group. When Daniel heard why the king was so angry, Daniel told him he would be able to tell the king about the meaning of his dream, but first he needed time to pray. That night God gave him the answer in a vision.

241

The Dream and its Meaning

Daniel 2

The next morning Daniel said to the king, "Don't kill the wise men. Only God can explain your dream. God has told me about it because he wants you to know his message.

"You dreamed about a huge statue.

Its head was made of gold, its chest and arms of silver, the middle part was bronze, the legs were iron, and the feet were of iron and clay mixed together.

"You saw a rock roll down the mountainside and smash the statue. Then the rock grew bigger until it filled the whole earth."

Then Daniel explained what the dream meant. "The statue is you. You are the head of gold. But after your kingdom is gone, another kingdom will take its place. It will be less powerful, just as silver is not as great as gold.

"Then the bronze kingdom will rule. It will be followed by another, like the

iron legs. Then the iron kingdom will divide and be like the mixture of iron and clay.

"The stone stands for a great kingdom that will destroy all the others. It will come from God."

The king was grateful to Daniel. King Nebuchadnezzar made Daniel a ruler assisted by his three friends.

— 242 —
"We Will Not Bow to Your Statue"

Daniel 3

Nebuchadnezzar built a big statue, ninety feet high and nine feet wide. He sent a message to the leaders in the country: "When you hear the band play, everyone must bow and worship the statue. Anyone who doesn't will be thrown into a hot furnace."

The band played, and everyone bowed to the statue. Daniel wasn't there, but Shadrach, Meshach, and Abednego refused to bow down.

Some of the government leaders came to the king and said, "Those young men who came as captives from Judah aren't bowing down to your statue. Are you going to let them get away with it?"

The king called the young men and yelled at them, "Don't you respect me? Don't you know I can throw you into the furnace?"

They answered quietly, "O king, even if you do put us into the furnace, our God will take care of us. Even if he should let us die, we would never worship anyone but our God. We will not bow to your statue."

— 243 —
How Many Men in the Furnace?

Daniel 3

When the three young men refused to bow to the statue, the king became even angrier. He shouted, "Heat up that furnace seven times hotter than before. Tie these men up, and throw them into the fire!"

The soldiers obeyed, but the fire was so hot that it burned them when they threw in the three men. As King Nebuchadnezzar watched, he saw something very strange. "I thought we put three men into the furnace. Now I see four men walking around in the flames. They don't even seem to be hurt by the fire."

The king came as close to the furnace as he could and called to the men, "Shadrach! Meshach! Abednego! You servants of the Most High God, come out of the furnace."

When the men stepped out, everyone could see that even their hair wasn't singed. King Nebuchadnezzar was so amazed that he made a new announcement. "I command that from now on, if anyone in this country says anything bad about God, he will be killed, and his house will be pulled down."

Then he promoted Shadrach, Meshach, and Abednego to higher positions in his government.

244
Another Strange Dream

Daniel 4

Later King Nebuchadnezzar had another strange dream. He told Daniel,

"I saw a tree so tall that everyone in the world could see it. It had beautiful leaves and fruit. An angel came and said, 'Cut down the tree. Leave the stump in the ground where it will be soaked with rain. Let this "tree" eat grass like an animal and have a mind like an animal's; then everyone will know how great God is.'"

Daniel knew what the dream meant, but he didn't want to tell the king.

The king begged him to tell, so finally Daniel said, "O king, you are the great tree. But your kingdom will be taken away, and for seven years you will act like an animal – soaked with rain, living outdoors, and eating grass. Only when you admit how great God is will you be healed and get your kingdom back."

Nothing happened for a year, and the

king refused to give God credit for the good things that happened to him. The angel said, "It's time for the dream to come true." Then all the terrible things in Nebuchadnezzar's dream took place.

After seven years, he began to praise and worship God. He got his throne back and told everyone about how wonderful God is.

— 245 —
The Mysterious Hand

Daniel 5

One of the kings after Nebuchadnezzar was Belshazzar. Once Belshazzar had a big party. Everyone got drunk and behaved foolishly. Belshazzar told his servants to bring in the silver and gold cups that had been taken from the Temple in Jerusalem. The king and his guests drank wine from the sacred cups and used them in a ceremony honouring their idols!

Suddenly they saw a hand writing some words on a wall. They were frightened, Belshazzar most of all. None of his wise men could read or explain the strange words.

The queen said, "Don't get so upset. Send for the man named Daniel. His God has given him a special ability to explain things like this."

Belshazzar said to Daniel, "If you can explain these words, I'll make you a rich man."

Daniel replied, "I don't want your money, but I will tell you what the handwriting means. God is telling you that you are not fit to rule. He is going to let your enemies capture the city."

The king gave Daniel gifts and made him an important official. But that night the enemy army sneaked into Babylon and killed Belshazzar.

246
Daniel Keeps on Praying

Daniel 6

The new king, Darius, noticed what a wise official Daniel was, so he gave Daniel an important job in his government. The more the king honoured Daniel, the more angry and jealous the other governors became. But no one could find any fault with Daniel because he was such an honest, hardworking man.

One reason Daniel was so successful was that he trusted and obeyed God. He prayed three times each day, worshipping God and asking him for wisdom.

Daniel's enemies said, "Maybe we can get him into trouble for praying."

They said to the king, "We think everyone should pray to you alone for the next thirty days, and if any man prays to anyone else, he should be thrown into a pit full of lions. We've written this down as a new law. Will you sign it?"

The king felt powerful and proud. Quickly he signed the law.

Daniel heard about the new law, but he still prayed to his God as usual. His enemies were spying on him. They saw him kneeling at his open window. "Now we have him!" they gloated.

247
Thrown to the Lions

Daniel 6

When Daniel's enemies saw him praying, they rushed to the king. "O king, didn't you make a law that anyone who prays to any god but you should be thrown to the lions?"

The king said, "Yes, and no one can change a Persian king's law."

Then the men said, "Well, Daniel is breaking your law. He prays to his God every day."

The king had never intended that Daniel should be punished for praying to the God of Israel. He tried to think of a way to get Daniel out of trouble, but the law couldn't be changed.

Daniel was arrested and thrown into the lion pit, and the opening was blocked. All that night the king couldn't sleep.

In the morning he hurried to the pit and called, "Daniel! Did your God keep you safe from the lions?"

Daniel answered, "I'm fine, sir. God sent an angel to keep the lions' mouths shut. I'm not even scratched!"

The king shouted, "Wonderful! Get him out of there!" And he threw the men who had made trouble for Daniel into the pit with their families, and the lions killed them all!

— 248 —
Daniel Prays for His Country

Daniel 9

King Darius said that everyone in his country should honour and worship the God of Daniel. He kept promoting Daniel, and when Darius died, the next king, Cyrus, did the same. Daniel had dreams that showed him that kingdoms would rise and fall but that God had good plans for his special people, the Israelites. The time of the Israelites' captivity in Babylon was almost over. Soon they would be able to return to the Land of Promise.

Daniel began to pray that God would lead his people back to Jerusalem, where they could begin to live in their own land once more. Daniel admitted to God that his people had been disobedient. "We don't really deserve your kindness. Please be good to us just because you are a merciful God."

He had been praying this way for three weeks, when suddenly the angel Gabriel came to make some wonderful promises to him. Not only would the people of Israel be able to go back home, Gabriel told him, but almost five hundred years later, God would send a Saviour to the world.

249
Back Home at Last

Ezra 1–3; Isaiah 44

Seventy years had passed since God's people were taken captive. The king who ruled them now was Cyrus. Almost two hundred years before he became king, God had mentioned his name in his messages to Isaiah! God had said Cyrus would be a kindhearted ruler who would help the captives return to their own land.

Cyrus said, "Everyone who wants to go is free to leave." He gave them money and sent back the gold and silver dishes that Nebuchadnezzar had stolen from the Temple. Almost fifty thousand people decided to make the trip, and they took many animals.

Joshua, the high priest, and Zerubbabel led the people and helped them get organized when they arrived in Judah. The first thing they did was to build an altar outside the ruins of the Temple. There they worshipped God and asked for his help as they settled down and rebuilt his house.

They laid the foundation stones; then they celebrated with songs of praise.

But the old men, who could remember seventy years back, cried. They shook their heads sadly and said, "It will never be as beautiful as the Temple Solomon built!"

250
The Most Beautiful Queen

Esther 1–2

Thousands of the Jews returned to Judah, but many stayed in Babylonia, which was now ruled by Persian kings. One of those kings was Xerxes. One day Xerxes had a huge party. The king got drunk and sent for his queen, Vashti: "Get over here! I want you to show the men at my party what a beautiful queen I have." The queen refused to show off for those drunken men.

This made the king terribly angry. His advisors said, "If you let the queen get away with this, all the women in the kingdom will start disobeying their husbands. Throw Vashti out, and get a queen who will show respect for Your Majesty."

The king agreed, but later he began to miss Vashti. Then his advisors put on a beauty contest. The winner would be Xerxes' new queen.

The one Xerxes chose was a beautiful Jewish girl named Esther. She and

her uncle, Mordecai, were captives from Jerusalem. Mordecai told Esther, "You'd better not tell the king you are a Jew."

The king was happy. He had the most beautiful woman in the country for his queen!

251
A Dangerous Law
Esther 2–3

One day Mordecai discovered a plot to kill Xerxes. Mordecai told Esther to warn the king. With the help of the warning the traitors were caught and punished. It was all written down in the court records, then forgotten.

Haman, the king's most powerful official, liked everyone to bow down to him. Mordecai refused to bow to Haman because, as a Jew, he believed he should bow only to God. This made Haman angry – with Mordecai and with all Jews.

Haman planned to get even. He said to the king, "These Israelite captives have their own rules and laws and refuse to obey yours. We'd better get rid of them. Declare that they must all be killed, and I'll pay a lot of money into your treasury."

The king agreed, and Haman made a terrible law – on a certain day in March, all citizens should kill all the Jews they could find. They could then take those Jews' possessions for their own. Haman sent messengers out all over the country to announce the law.

being killed in March with the rest of our people. Perhaps this is why you were chosen as queen – so you could help your fellow Jews."

Esther asked Mordecai to pray for her and to start prayer meetings all over the city. "I will go to see the king. If he kills me – at least I will have tried to help my people." While all the Jews were praying for Esther, she worked out a plan to try to convince her husband, the king, to help the Jews get out of danger.

When Mordecai heard about it, he was brokenhearted. Mordecai wondered what he could possibly do to save his people.

252
Mordecai Asks Esther to Help

Esther 4

Queen Esther didn't know about Haman's law. When she heard that her uncle was outside the palace crying, she sent someone to find out what was wrong. Mordecai sent a message back, telling her about the trouble the Jews were in and asking her to get the king to help.

She replied, "The king is likely to kill anyone who goes to see him without an invitation, unless he is feeling kind and holds out his sceptre. It would be dangerous for me to go."

Mordecai sent another message: "You are queen, but that won't keep you from

---

253
A Sneaky Plot

Esther 5–7

It was dangerous for Esther to go to the king without being invited. But her life was saved when the king held out his sceptre to her! He said, "What can I do for you?" Esther replied, "I want you and Haman to come to a banquet tonight." The king accepted, and they had a fine dinner. The king asked again, "What do you want from me?"

Esther answered, "I want you both to return tomorrow for another banquet."

Haman bragged about his invitation to his family

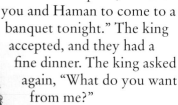

and said, "I would be completely happy if it weren't for Mordecai."

Haman's wife said, "Build a gallows and get the king's permission to hang Mordecai tomorrow. Then you can enjoy the banquet."

That night, the king found the record of how Mordecai had saved his life. He realized he had never rewarded Mordecai. When Haman came to see him, to ask about killing Mordecai, the king spoke first. "Haman, how could I honour someone special?"

Haman assumed the king meant him. He said, "Give him a robe and a crown. Let him ride your horse through the city. And have a prince shout, 'This is how the king honours someone who is worthy.'"

"Excellent! Do all these things for Mordecai!"

254
The Brave Queen Saves Her People

Esther 7–10

What a shock for Haman! That night he and the king went to Esther's second banquet. Again the king asked Esther what she wanted. Esther said, "O king, please save my life and the lives of all the Jews in your kingdom, for we are to be killed."

"What do you mean?" the king cried. "Who would dare to threaten your life?"

"Haman has ordered all Jews to be killed – and I am one of them!" she answered.

The king was terribly angry and left the room to think about the problem. Haman was afraid. He threw himself across Esther's couch to beg for mercy.

The king came back in and thought Haman was trying to hurt Esther, so the king ordered Haman's death.

Haman was hanged on the gallows that he had built for Mordecai!

The king gave Haman's job as prime minister to Mordecai, but he could not change the law about killing Jews.

So Esther said, "Since you cannot change the law, will you make another one permitting the Jews to fight back?"

Xerxes said yes, and when the Jews were attacked, they fought back, and their lives were saved.

255
Trouble for the Builders

Ezra 4

The Jews who had returned to Jerusalem kept working on the Temple. The Samaritans, who had been living in Judah while the Jews were in Babylon, were spying on them. They were not true worshippers of God. When they saw that the Temple in Jerusalem was being rebuilt, they pretended they wanted to help.

Joshua and Zerubbabel didn't trust the Samaritans. They said, "No, thanks! We can do the job by ourselves."

The Samaritans didn't like this, so they tried to discourage the workers. They wrote to Artaxerxes, who had become king of Persia when Xerxes died.

They lied about the Israelites. "O king, when these people get the Temple and the city rebuilt, they will not be loyal to you. They won't pay taxes. They have always been troublemakers wherever they live."

After a while the Samaritans got the king's answer. "It seems the people of Jerusalem have often caused trouble. Tell them to stop building immediately. If I change my mind later, I'll let them know."

This was what the Samaritans wanted. They showed the king's letter to the builders. "You are ordered to stop your work right now!" So long as Artaxerxes lived, the men of Judah did nothing more to restore their Temple.

256
Ezra Comes to Teach

Ezra 7–10

Ezra was a religious leader among the prisoners in Babylon. He knew a great deal about the Law of Moses. He wondered who would teach the people who had returned to Judah about the Law. How would they know how to worship when they got the Temple finished?

He decided to be their teacher, so he asked Artaxerxes for permission to leave. The king let him go along with a group that included priests, Levites, singers, and Temple musicians.

The king gave them money and other treasures, which they guarded very carefully on the long trip back to Judah.

Artaxerxes admitted that he was letting all these people go because he was afraid of their God and didn't want to be punished for keeping the Israelites as captives.

When Ezra arrived in Judah, he worked hard to teach God's Law to the people. He was upset to find that Israelite men were marrying heathen women from tribes around them.

Ezra prayed, confessing the sin of his people and pleading for forgiveness. Then the people were sorry about what they had done, and they stopped marrying heathen women.

257
The King is Kind to Nehemiah

Nehemiah 1–2

King Artaxerxes had a Jewish servant, Nehemiah, whom he liked and trusted. One day Nehemiah asked some friends who had recently been to Jerusalem, "Are the city walls being rebuilt as we had hoped?"

The men told him the work was going ahead very slowly and that the walls of Jerusalem were still in

ruins. This worried Nehemiah. The king noticed. "What is the matter, Nehemiah?" he asked.

"Your Majesty, I am unhappy because my countrymen who returned to Judah have not made much progress with the rebuilding. My beautiful city is still in ruins after all these years. Sir, would you let me go back to Judah and see that the work gets done?"

The king said, "All right, you may go. Let me know when you will be back." And he gave Nehemiah letters to the rulers of the countries Nehemiah would travel through, asking them to let Nehemiah pass safely.

The rulers let him travel through their territory, but two of them – Sanballat and Tobiah – weren't pleased about it. They didn't like anyone to help the Israelites who were resettling Judah.

258
The Jews Work on the City Walls

Nehemiah 2–6

When Nehemiah got to Jerusalem, he knew that enemies, like Sanballat and Tobiah, would not want him to succeed in his project. He called his workers together and told them his plans. "We must build the walls first so that we can keep our enemies out of the city while we do other building work. Come on, let's get it done!"

The people got busy right away. Sanballat and Tobiah saw what was happening, and they tried to discourage the workers:

"Why, those walls are so weak, the weight of an ant would crumble them!"

"Look at those crazy Jews! How do they think they can build a wall around the city without any good stones?"

But the people kept on working. Their enemies saw that they would have to attack. Nehemiah heard about their plan and told his workers to carry weapons all the time.

Sanballat and Tobiah changed their minds about attacking, but from then on, half the Israelites stood guard while the other half worked on the wall. And every one of them carried a sword.

Just fifty-two days after the people started working, the wall was finished!

259
The Temple is Finished at Last!

Ezra 5–6; Haggai

Once Artaxerxes stopped the work on the Temple, the people began building houses for themselves. They lost interest in the Temple. Even after Artaxerxes died, they didn't bother to ask the new ruler, Darius II, for permission to start the Temple work again.

Their selfishness disappointed God. He warned them through his messengers, the prophets Haggai and Zechariah.

Haggai said, "You are neglecting the Temple and thinking only of your own comfort. God's house is still in ruins, so get to work!"

The people were ashamed. They started work on the Temple immediately. The Samaritans said, "Who said you could work on the Temple again?"

The leaders replied, "King Cyrus sent us to take care of God's house."

The Samaritans wrote to Darius and said, "Did King Cyrus really tell these people to rebuild the Temple?"

Darius checked and found Cyrus's decree. He wrote, "You Samaritans must let the Israelites get on with their work, or I will punish you. And you must give them part of the tax money you owe me."

So the people of Judah were able to finish the Temple and celebrate the feast of Passover in their new house of worship.

— 260 —
Joyful Celebration
Nehemiah 8–13

The time of captivity for the people of Judah was over. Many of them had returned to live in their own land. The walls of Jerusalem were built, and the Temple had been rebuilt, so they could worship and serve God in his own house. They had even brought back the gold and silver bowls and cups and other treasures that had been stolen from the old Temple.

The Israelites had several celebrations to show their joy. When the walls were finished, they had a parade around the top of the wall. Then they marched to the Temple and made sacrifices to God.

They also had a thanksgiving celebration called the Festival of Trumpets. During that time Ezra read the Book of the Law aloud to everyone. He read for hours, and the people stood and listened. They all told God they were sorry for disobeying him and that they would try to do better.

Next, they signed a paper, making promises: "We will obey God, not mingle with the heathen tribes, not marry ungodly women, give the Lord a tenth of our money and grain, and keep the Sabbath day a holy day of rest."

— 261 —
Many Years of Trouble

Secular History

The people of Israel were back home, but they were not really free. They paid taxes to the Persian kings, who still ruled them. During the next four hundred years, one government followed another, but the Jews were always servants. The Greeks, the Egyptians, the Arameans – each ruled the Jews for a time. Then for about a hundred years they became free again, while a family of Jewish leaders, called the Maccabees, kept invaders out of Judah. Once more the people could worship God in their Temple.

But soon the Jews neglected to worship God and fought among themselves. So God let another foreign army conquer them. This time it was the Romans. The Roman emperor sent a soldier named Herod to be king of Judah. Herod was cruel, and the people hated him. He tried to make friends with the people by rebuilding the Temple, which by now was five hundred years old and in bad condition. Herod spent nine years rebuilding it, and made the Temple really beautiful.

But the Jews were still unhappy under Roman rule. They longed for a great leader to come and free them!

THE NEW TESTAMENT

— 262 —
A Surprise for Zechariah

Luke 1

Zechariah was a priest in the newly rebuilt Temple. He and his wife, Elizabeth, were disappointed that they had had no children and that now they were too old. The priests took turns doing each task in the Temple. One day it was Zechariah's turn to burn incense in the Holy Place. As he did this, he saw an angel beside the altar.

The angel said, "Don't be afraid, Zechariah. I have good news. You and Elizabeth are going to have a baby boy! You must name him John and bring him up in a certain way: he must never drink any wine.

"The Holy Spirit will live in him. He will bring people back to God and get them ready for the promised Messiah."

Zechariah was amazed. He said, "How can this happen? My wife and I are too old to have a baby."

"Because you don't believe," the angel replied, "you will become unable to speak until after the baby is born!" When Zechariah came out of the Holy Place, he couldn't say a word. But he showed everyone by his hand motions what he had seen and heard in the Temple.

— 263 —
A Promise from an Angel

Luke 1

God sent the angel Gabriel to Nazareth with a message for a young woman named Mary. Mary was a virgin; that is, she had never slept with a man. She was engaged to be married to Joseph, a local carpenter.

Mary was startled when the angel suddenly appeared in her room. Gabriel said, "Mary, you have been chosen for a great honour." Mary was troubled by his words.

He continued, "Don't be afraid. You will soon become pregnant, and when your baby boy is born, you will name him Jesus. He will be very great and will have the throne of his ancestor David. His kingdom will never end."

Mary was puzzled. She said to Gabriel, "How can I have a baby? I'm a virgin!"

The angel replied, "You will become pregnant by the power of the Holy Spirit. Your baby will be the Son of God. Your cousin Elizabeth is pregnant, too, even though she is beyond the age for having babies. Nothing that God promises is impossible!"

Mary answered joyfully, "I'm God's servant, and I'm glad to do whatever he wants me to do."

264
Elizabeth Has a Baby Boy

Luke 1

When Elizabeth was about six months pregnant, Mary visited her. As Mary entered the house, Elizabeth's baby leaped inside her, and Elizabeth was filled with the Holy Spirit.

She said to Mary, "You are a fortunate woman. God has chosen you because you believe and are willing to obey."

Then Mary said, "Praise God because he has chosen me, a simple village girl. He's going to put down rulers and lift up lowly people. He has promised to be faithful to Abraham's children forever."

Mary went home after three months. Elizabeth had her baby, and she and Zechariah did as the angel had told them.

The neighbours thought they should name the baby after Zechariah, but Elizabeth said, "No, he is to be named John."

They asked Zechariah, and he wrote, "His name is John!" Immediately Zechariah got his speech back again!

He said, "The Lord is going to send us a Saviour. My child shall be a prophet of God, preparing the way before the Saviour."

Once John grew up, he spent a lot of time in the desert, until it was time for him to speak God's messages.

265
God Sends His Son

Luke 2

Joseph and Mary got married. Shortly before the baby came, the Roman emperor said everyone must go to his or her family's hometown to be counted. Joseph and Mary both came from David's family, so they had to register in Bethlehem.

Bethlehem was crowded with people, and all the inns were full. The only space they could find was in a shed with some animals.

That night Mary's baby was born. She wrapped her little boy in warm clothes and put him in a manger.

At first, the only people who knew what had happened were some shepherds. They saw many angels in the sky and heard them say, "Glory to God! Peace on earth! A Saviour has been born today in Bethlehem. You will find him warmly wrapped and lying in a manger!"

After the angels had disappeared, the shepherds said, "Let's go and see!"

They found the little baby with Mary and Joseph. Everything was just as the angels had said. After they had visited the baby, the shepherds went out and told everyone the news.

Mary thought about what had happened and wondered what it all meant.

— 266 —
Simeon and Anna

Luke 2

The Law told new parents to dedicate their first baby boy to God. When the baby was eight days old, the parents were to name him. Mary and Joseph named their baby Jesus because that is what the angel had told Mary to do.

Later, they travelled to Jerusalem and took baby Jesus to the Temple. At the Temple they saw an old man named Simeon. He spent a lot of time in the Temple because God had told him he would not die until he had seen the baby who would become the Messiah – the Saviour.

As soon as Simeon saw the baby Jesus, he knew this was the One. He took Jesus from Mary and prayed, "O Lord, now I can die in peace. I have seen the baby who will bring your salvation to the world."

Anna lived in the Temple. She was very old and had been a prophet for many years. She, too, recognized Jesus as the Messiah. She thanked God for the Saviour, then hurried to tell everyone she met that the Messiah had been born.

267
The Wise Men

Matthew 2

Far away in another country, some wise men saw a bright new star. They knew it was a sign that a great king had been born. They wanted to take gifts to him, so they decided to follow the star until they found him.

After they had travelled for many days, they arrived at Jerusalem. They asked everyone, "Where is the new king of the Jews? We have been following his star because we want to worship him."

King Herod heard about them, and he was worried. Was some new king going to take away his throne? Could these foreigners be talking about the Jewish Messiah?

Herod asked the wise men when they had first seen the star. He told them to go ahead and find the baby king. "Then come back and tell me where he is, so I can worship him too," Herod said.

The star led the wise men to the house where Mary, Joseph, and Jesus were staying. The men bowed to Jesus and gave him valuable gifts – gold, frankincense, and myrrh.

Then they had a dream in which God said, "Don't go back to Herod. Take a different road home."

268
Hiding from Herod

Matthew 2; Luke 2

When King Herod found that the wise men had left without reporting to him, he was angry. He sent soldiers to Bethlehem to kill all little boys younger than two years old.

But God sent an angel to warn Joseph. "Take Mary and Jesus to Egypt, and stay there until I say it is safe to come back."

Joseph kept his family in Egypt until King Herod died. Then Joseph had a dream in which God said, "You can safely go back now." They went to live in Nazareth, where they had lived before.

Jesus grew to be a fine, strong boy. Once, when he was twelve, he was in Jerusalem with his parents for the Passover. When the group from Nazareth started home, Jesus stayed behind.

After a while Mary and Joseph missed him and went back to look for him. They found him in the Temple, talking with the teachers of the Law, who were surprised by his wisdom.

Mary said, "Son, how could you cause us such worry?"

Jesus answered, "I thought you would know I'd be in my Father's house!" Then he went home with them and was always an obedient son.

— 269 —
John Baptizes Jesus
Matthew 3; Mark 1; Luke 3

John and Jesus were cousins. John had been chosen to prepare people to receive the Messiah and to announce his coming. John told the people, "You must be sorry for your sins and take care of the poor and the hungry. I baptize people in water, but the Messiah will baptize you with the Holy Spirit."

People asked John, "Aren't you the Messiah?"

"No," he answered. "He will come later. He's so great that I'm not worthy even to untie his shoes!"

One day Jesus came to the Jordan River. John called out, "Look! There is the Lamb of God – the Messiah!"

Jesus asked John to baptize him. John answered, "No! I'm the one who should be baptized by you!" But Jesus insisted. So John baptized Jesus in the river.

Just as Jesus came up out of the water, the heavens opened. God's Holy Spirit, looking like a dove, came down and lighted on Jesus. Then the voice spoke from heaven: "This is my dear Son, whom I love. I am greatly pleased with him."

— 270 —
Satan Tempts Jesus
Matthew 4; Mark 1; Luke 4

After Jesus was baptized, he went into the wilderness. He ate nothing for forty days and nights. While Jesus was weak from hunger, Satan came to him. Satan said, "If you're really the Son of God, turn these stones into bread."

Jesus answered, "The Scriptures say we don't live just by eating bread. We live by obeying every word God says to us."

Satan took Jesus onto the roof of the Temple in Jerusalem. Satan said, "Jump off! That will prove to everyone that you are the Son of God. The Scriptures say God will send angels to keep you from being hurt."

"What it really says," Jesus answered, "is that we should not test God in such a foolish way!"

Satan tried once more. He took Jesus to the top of a high mountain. They could see all the kingdoms of the world.

Satan said, "I'll give you these kingdoms to rule if you kneel down and worship me."

Jesus said, "Get out of here, Satan. The Scriptures say, 'You must worship and obey the Lord God, and not anyone else!'"

Satan gave up and went away.

— 271 —
Jesus' First Miracle
John 2

Jesus asked some men to leave their work and travel around with him. He taught them important things, so they were called his disciples. One day he and his disciples were invited to a wedding in Cana. Jesus' mother, Mary, was there too. Unfortunately, the wine was all gone long before the celebration was over.

Mary spoke to Jesus about it, but he said, "Don't expect me to do anything about it. It isn't time yet for me to do miracles." Mary didn't argue with him, but she said to the serving men, "If Jesus tells you to do something, do it."

There were six large waterpots in the kitchen. Jesus said to the servants, "Fill each of these pots with water." The servants obeyed. "Now," Jesus said, "take

some of it to the master of the feast."

The master tasted what they gave him. "This is excellent wine!" he exclaimed. He said to the bridegroom, "Most people give their guests the best wine first, then the cheaper wine. But you have saved the very best wine until last!"

That was the first miracle Jesus did.

—— 272 ——
How to Be Born Again

John 3

More and more people began to listen to Jesus. Some thought he might be the Messiah, but the Pharisees, who were the main church leaders, didn't like him at all.

One Pharisee, named Nicodemus, was different. He visited Jesus secretly, late one night. Nicodemus said, "Teacher, I believe you have come from God."

Jesus said, "Nicodemus, if you want to be in the kingdom of God, you must be born again – in a heavenly way."

Nicodemus said, "How can an adult be born again like a little baby?"

Jesus replied, "This is a different kind of birth. God's Holy Spirit makes your spirit alive, and that is like being born into a new life. You can't see the Spirit doing this. He is like the wind – invisible but powerful."

"Please explain," said Nicodemus.

Jesus said, "The Son of Man has come from heaven and will return there. I am like the brass serpent that Moses lifted up in the wilderness. I'll be lifted up so people can be saved."

Then Jesus said, "For God loved the world so much that he gave his only Son so that anyone who believes in him shall not die but live forever."

273
King Herod – John's Powerful Enemy

Matthew 14; Mark 6; Luke 3; John 3

One day John the Baptist's followers said, "Master, Jesus is becoming famous. Many people are leaving you to follow him." John said, "That's the way it should be. Jesus should become greater, and I should become less important."

Then John did something dangerous. He criticized King Herod for marrying Herodias, who was his brother's wife. This made Herod so angry that he put John in jail. After a while, Herod realized what a good man John was. Herod kept him in jail, but he protected him. Much later, the king was giving a feast. Herodias's young daughter, Salome, danced for Herod and pleased him so much that he offered to give her anything she wanted! Salome asked her mother what she should ask for. Herodias had never forgiven John for speaking against her marriage. Herodias said, "Ask for John's head on a platter!"

When Herod heard Salome's request, he was sorry he had made such a foolish offer. But he couldn't break his promise, so he ordered his soldiers to cut off John's head. John's disciples came and buried his body.

274
The Woman at the Well

John 4

As Jesus sat by a well in Samaria, a woman of the village came with her pitcher. Jesus asked her for a drink. She said, "That's a surprise. You Jews don't usually speak to Samaritans."

Jesus said, "If you knew who I am, you would ask me for living water!"

"Living water?" she echoed. "You don't have a rope or a pail. How could you get water?"

Jesus replied, "The well water leaves you thirsty. But the water I give satisfies you forever."

"Then give me some," she said.

"First go and get your husband," said Jesus.

She hesitated. "… I don't have a husband."

Jesus said, "You have had too many husbands. And you are not married to the man you live with now."

The woman was embarrassed and changed the subject. "Why do you Jews worship in one place and we Samaritans in another?"

Jesus answered, "It's not important where we worship but how. Remember, salvation will come through the Jews."

"When the Messiah comes," she answered, "he will tell us everything."

"I am the Messiah!" he said.

The woman called everyone to come and meet Jesus. He preached to them for two days.

275
Jesus Heals a Sick Boy
John 4

Many people in the Samaritan village believed that Jesus was the Saviour. Then Jesus and his friends moved on to Galilee. They stopped in Cana. A rich government officer from Capernaum approached Jesus and begged him for help. The officer said, "My little boy is very sick and about to die. Please, come to Capernaum and heal him."

Jesus sighed. "You people always want to see miracles before you will believe in me."

The child's father said again, "Please, sir! Come and heal him before it is too late!"

Jesus said, "Go back home now. Your little son has been healed!"

The officer believed Jesus and started for home. His servants hurried out to meet him. "Oh, Master, good news! Your son is not going to die. He has recovered!"

The happy father asked his servants, "When did he start to get better?"

They answered, "About one o'clock yesterday afternoon." The boy's father realized that was the exact time at which Jesus had told him his son was healed.

276
From Fishermen to Followers
Matthew 4; Mark 1; Luke 5

Jesus was walking by the Sea of Galilee. He watched the fishermen and noticed two brothers, Simon and Andrew. Jesus called to them, "If you were working with me, you would be fishing for men instead of fish!"

He said the same thing to two other brothers, James and John, who were fishing with their father,

Zebedee. All four brothers listened to what Jesus was teaching.

Such crowds came to hear Jesus that he hardly had room to move. He got into Simon's boat and said, "Push the boat out a little way, and I'll speak to the people from there."

After Jesus had finished preaching, he said, "Now let's go out where it's deeper, and you can get some fish."

Simon answered, "We tried all night but couldn't find any. But if you say so, we'll try again."

They threw their nets out, and they caught so many fish that the nets broke from the weight. They were awed and a little bit afraid at what Jesus had done.

Jesus asked both pairs of brothers to leave their fishing business and become his disciples. All four men came immediately.

277

Jesus Heals the Sick

Matthew 8; Mark 1; Luke 4

Each town had a small place of worship called a synagogue. Whenever a famous speaker came to town, he was invited to teach there. The people of Capernaum asked Jesus to speak in their synagogue.

While he was there, a demon-possessed man called out, "Go away, Jesus of Nazareth! You've just come to make trouble for us because you are the Son of God!"

Jesus said, "Be still! Come out of him!" The demon threw the man to the ground, but it left him alone after that. From then on the man was normal.

The crowd was excited. "Imagine that! Jesus has the power to make demons come out of people!"

Then Simon took Jesus and the other followers to his home. They found that Simon's wife's mother was very sick with a high fever. Jesus went to her bedside and told the fever to leave her. She felt better immediately and got up and cooked a meal for Jesus and his friends.

That evening many other sick and demon-possessed people came and asked to be healed. Jesus healed each one.

— 278 —
Down Through the Roof!

Matthew 9; Mark 2; Luke 5

A paralyzed man wanted Jesus to heal him. Four of his closest friends made a kind of stretcher-bed, and they carried him to the house where Jesus was staying. When they saw the huge crowds, they decided to lift the stretcher up onto the flat roof and lower their friend into the room where Jesus was healing people.

They made a hole in the roof, then carefully eased the stretcher down until their friend was lying right in front of Jesus!

Jesus was pleased when he saw the faith of the man's friends. Jesus said to the paralyzed man, "I forgive your sins."

The religious leaders, who didn't like Jesus, said, "Who does he think he is? Only God can forgive sin."

Jesus knew what they were thinking. He said, "Which do you think is harder – to forgive sin or to heal the body? Well, I'll do both!" He said to the paralyzed man, "Stand up; you are well. Now go on home."

The man jumped to his feet, picked up the stretcher, and hurried home. Everyone was absolutely amazed!

— 279 —
Jesus and the Sabbath

John 5

One Sabbath day Jesus passed Bethesda Pool. Many sick people waited there because when the water moved, the first person into the pool was healed. A man was there who had been sick for thirty-eight years. He was too weak to move quickly into the pool. Jesus healed him and said, "Get up, roll up your mat, and go home."

When the religious leaders saw the man, they said, "Carrying that mat is work. You are breaking the Law by working on the Sabbath."

The man replied, "I don't know his name, but the man who healed me told me to carry it."

Later Jesus saw the man again and warned him not to go on being a sinner. Then the man told the leaders who had healed him.

The leaders scolded Jesus for not respecting the Sabbath laws. Jesus said, "My Father does good things for people no matter what day it is. I do as he does."

The leaders were shocked that Jesus called God his own father. Jesus continued, "If you don't honour the Son, you dishonour the Father. Whoever listens to what I say and believes God sent me shall have life forever."

—— 280 ——
The Twelve Special Disciples
Mark 2–3; Luke 6

Jesus and his followers were walking through a field on the Sabbath. Some of them were hungry, so they picked some grain, rubbed the husks off, and ate the kernels. The Pharisees said that rubbing the husks from the grain was like doing farm work, which was forbidden on the Sabbath.

Jesus said, "I have been made master of the Sabbath. I should know what is permitted and what is not!"

This made the leaders even angrier. They began to plan to kill Jesus. Jesus

took his followers back to the Sea of Galilee, and he healed many sick people.

One day Jesus went alone into the desert to pray. When he returned, he chose twelve of his followers to be an inner circle of companions and helpers. They would travel with him, preach, and help heal the sick.

The twelve special disciples were Peter (the new name Jesus gave Simon the fisherman), Andrew (Peter's brother), James and his brother John, Philip, Bartholomew, Thomas, Matthew (who had been a tax collector), another man named James, Thaddaeus, Simon, and Judas Iscariot.

281
Jesus Preaches on a Mountain

Matthew 5; Luke 6

Everywhere Jesus went, people crowded around him. He decided the best way to speak to so many people was to climb up high on a hill. That way everyone would be able to see and hear what went on.

One time when he taught on a mountain, he was teaching his disciples, but everyone wanted to hear.

We call this the Sermon on the Mount. Jesus told the people how to be happy and enjoy God's blessing.

Be humble, not proud and stubborn.

Be sorry for your sins.

Be meek and listen to other people's opinions.

Be eager to do right.

Be kind to everyone else.

Be pure in your hearts, thinking only about good things.

Be peaceable and help others not to quarrel.

Then he said something that sounds very strange: "Be glad when others are mean to you because you believe in me and obey me! God will give you a great reward if you suffer for being my followers."

282

Jesus Tells How We Should Live

Matthew 6; Luke 6

In his rules for being happy, Jesus said a lot about being good. Here is a list of some of his instructions:

Be like a bright light, helping people see how good God is.

Do all the good things God told Moses in the Law.

Do not hate anyone, for hatred is like murder in the heart.

Settle your arguments quickly.

Men and women must have only pure thoughts about one another.

Married couples must not get divorced.

If you make a serious promise, you must keep it.

Be generous with others, even if they treat you unfairly.

Be just as nice to your enemies as you are to your friends.

Don't show off when you do generous things for others.

Don't show off when you pray, but do it privately.

Give your money generously to people in need, and God will take care of your needs.

Don't worry about what is going to happen. God is in control of your life.

283
Two Different Houses

Matthew 7; Luke 6

Jesus told his listeners not to be too quick to criticise other people but to check up on their own lives too. He promised that when they asked for God's help, he would always answer their call.

One of the most important things Jesus said was, "Do for other people the things you would like them to do for you!"

Jesus told a story. He said, "If you listen to what I say and obey my rules, you will be like a man who built his house on a rock. Heavy rainstorms came, the wind blew, and floodwater washed against his house; but it stood firm because it was built on a solid foundation.

"But if you hear what I tell you and do not pay any attention to my instructions, you will be like a man who built his house on sand. When the rain and wind and floods came, his house fell down with a mighty crash. It was a complete wreck because it had a poor foundation."

All the people who heard Jesus talk were surprised at how well he taught. They said, "We think God has given him authority to speak."

284
Jesus Shows Great Power
Matthew 8; Luke 7

A Roman who was friendly to the Jews paid to have a synagogue built in Capernaum. The Roman's servant became very sick, so the Roman sent word to Jesus asking him to come and heal his servant.

Even before Jesus got there, the Roman hurried out to meet him. "Master," he said, "I'm not good enough to have you enter my home. You can heal my servant without seeing him. Just speak the word, and he will be well."

Jesus said to the people around him, "This man has more faith than any Jew I know!" And he said to the Roman, "Go home. Your servant is healed."

When the man got home, he found the servant entirely well.

Later, Jesus saw a funeral procession in Nain. A widow's only son had died, and she was heartbroken. Jesus' heart was touched. He said to her, "Don't cry." Jesus stopped the procession and touched the casket. "Young man! Come back to life!"

The boy sat up and was able to talk and walk. Jesus led him to his mother. Everyone was amazed. People said, "This man is a great prophet. He can do the works of God!"

285
Showing Love to Jesus
Luke 7

One day a Pharisee invited Jesus to dinner. A sinful woman came to see Jesus. She brought an expensive jar of perfume. She was crying because she was sorry about her sins. Her tears fell on Jesus' feet, and she wiped them away with her hair. Then she poured the perfume on his feet to show her love and respect for him.

Simon the Pharisee thought Jesus couldn't be a prophet, or he would have known how bad the woman was and wouldn't be letting her touch him.

Jesus knew what Simon was thinking. Jesus said, "Simon, if a man lends fifty silver coins to one person and five hundred silver coins to another and then tells them they don't have to pay the money back, which debtor will love him more?"

Simon answered, "The one who owes him the larger amount."

Jesus said, "When I came to your house today, you didn't wash the dust from my feet – but this woman washed them with her tears. You didn't give me a kiss of greeting – but she kissed my feet. You didn't give me oil for my head – but she poured expensive perfume on my feet.

"She is a sinful woman, but I am forgiving her sins because she loves me so much."

— 286 —

A Story About Money

Luke 12

A man called to Jesus from the crowd, "Master, I wish you would tell my brother to divide our father's money fairly."

Jesus replied, "Don't ask me to settle your arguments! Besides, money won't make you happy.

"Listen. One year a farmer had such good crops that he became rich. His barns were full, so he built bigger ones.

The farmer thought he would be able to relax and have fun. He thought he'd be so rich that he'd not ever have to worry about money again!

"But that night God warned him: 'You are a fool! Tonight you will die, and then what will become of your riches?'"

Jesus said, "Don't waste time worrying about money, clothes, or food. Birds don't plant crops and build barns, yet God provides food for them. Aren't you more valuable to God than birds?

"And the flowers don't make cloth and sew clothes for themselves – but see how beautifully God dresses them! If God takes care of flowers, won't he take care of you? Spend most of your time thinking about God, and he will give you everything else you need!"

287
A Story About Seeds
Matthew 13; Mark 4; Luke 8

Jesus told stories that taught lessons, like this one: "A farmer went out to plant his seed. Some seed fell on the path. People walked on it, and birds flew down and ate it.

"Some of the seed fell on rocky soil. It started to grow, but there wasn't enough dirt to nourish the roots, so the little plants died.

"Some seed fell among weeds. The weeds were stronger than the grain seedlings, and the seedlings died.

"And some seed fell on good, rich soil. It grew tall and strong. At harvest time the farmer reaped a hundred times more than he had planted!"

The disciples asked him what the story meant. Jesus said, "The seeds are God's words. Some of his messages come to hard hearts, and the devil steals them away.

"Some of the messages come to shallow hearts. These people believe for a while, but then they lose interest. Some people's hearts are like a weed patch – other interests come in and crowd out God's truth. But some people are like the rich soil. They listen and believe God's words. Then the message grows and produces fruit – many times more fruit than was 'planted'!"

288
A Story About Faith

Matthew 13; Mark 4

Jesus said, "A mustard seed is tiny, but it grows into a very large plant. Faith is like that. If you believe even a little bit, your faith can grow and become strong." Then he said, "Once a farmer planted some good seed in a field. But some enemies came into his field and planted weeds among his good seeds. The weeds grew big and strong along with the good grain. The farmer's servants said, 'Master, did you know your field has a lot of weeds among the grain?'

"'Yes,' he said, 'An enemy did that.'

"'Shouldn't we pull up the weeds?' they asked.

"'If you do that,' he replied, 'you will pull up grain along with the weeds. Wait until harvest time. Then the reapers can separate the weeds from the grain.'

"That's the way it is with my kingdom. The good seed is like the people who have faith in me. The weeds are like those whom Satan has planted among my people. But one day the angels will take out all my true people. Then the ones who are wicked unbelievers will be destroyed."

289
Two Wonderful Miracles

Matthew 8; Mark 4–5; Luke 8

Jesus and his disciples were crossing the Sea of Galilee when a terrible storm blew up. The disciples thought the boat would sink. Jesus was sleeping soundly despite the storm. The disciples woke him up, yelling, "Master! Save us or we'll all drown!"

Jesus got up and spoke to the wind and the waves. "Stop! Be still!" Instantly the wind stopped and the sea was calm.

Jesus said, "Why were you afraid? You don't have much faith!"

On the other side of the lake they saw a man who had evil spirits living in him. He was naked, and he screamed and hurt himself with stones. Everyone in town was afraid of him.

The demon in the man cried out to Jesus, "Don't hurt me! I'm one of the many demons here. Let us go into the pigs over there."

Jesus said, "All right. Leave the man, and go into the pigs."

When they did, the large herd of pigs jumped into the lake and was drowned.

The man sat quietly with Jesus, acting perfectly normally. He wanted to join Jesus' group, but Jesus said, "No. Go home and tell your family and friends what has happened to you."

290
Jesus Gives Health and Strength

Matthew 9; Mark 5; Luke 8

Jairus was a religious leader. He begged Jesus to come to his home and heal his twelve-year-old daughter, who was dying. Jesus agreed, but on the way, a woman who had been sick for twelve years reached out and touched Jesus' robe. Immediately she was healed.

Jesus knew something had happened. Jesus asked his disciples, "Who touched me?"

They said, "Master, many people are bumping against you!"

Jesus said, "This was different. I felt healing strength go out from me."

The woman admitted that she was the one and that she had been healed. Jesus said, "You are well because you believed in me!"

As the group came near Jairus's house, a messenger came and said, "Sir, your little girl is dead."

Jesus said to Jairus, "Don't worry. She'll be all right. She's only sleeping."

The mourners were sure she was dead, and they laughed at Jesus. He took Peter, James, John, and the child's parents into the bedroom. Jesus held the girl's hand and said, "Little girl, get up!"

She jumped up, completely well!

291
Blind Men Can See

Matthew 9

As he left Jairus's house, Jesus noticed two blind men following him. One of them called, "Please take pity on me, O Son of David!" Jesus said to them, "Do you really believe I can heal your blindness?"

"Yes, Lord," they answered eagerly.

Jesus touched their eyes, and they could see clearly. He told them not to talk about what had happened to them, but they just couldn't keep quiet. They told their story everywhere.

That same day Jesus saw a man who could not say a word because a demon controlled his tongue. Jesus drove the demon out of the man, and the man could speak again. Everyone was amazed.

But the Pharisees were jealous of Jesus' success and fame. They said, "He can drive out demons only because he himself is demon-possessed!" But we know Jesus could do miracles because he was the Son of God!

Jesus kept on preaching, teaching, and healing throughout the countryside. He told his disciples, "All around us the harvest is ready, but we don't have enough people to help with the harvest. Let's pray for more workers."

— 292 —

The Disciples Tell the Good News

Matthew 10; Mark 6; Luke 9

Jesus wanted everyone to hear the Good News about being born again and being forgiven. He sent his twelve special disciples out to teach and preach his message. Jesus gave them the ability to heal the sick and set people free from demons. They could even raise the dead!

Jesus said, "Not everyone will receive you warmly. Some will be cruel to you. But even if they hurt your bodies, they can't harm your spirits.

"Don't take money, food, extra clothing, or shoes with you. God will give you what you need.

"You will be like the sparrows. God feeds them, and you are much more important than sparrows, so you can be sure God will provide everything you need.

"When people receive you kindly, give God's blessing to their homes. But if people treat you badly, just leave their town and don't have anything to do with them.

"Represent me wherever you go. If you try to hold on to your lives, you will lose them. But if you are willing to spend your lives serving me – even if you should die – you will be saving your lives for eternity."

293

Jesus Feeds a Crowd

Matthew 14; Mark 6; Luke 9; John 6

Jesus' disciples went out and preached the gospel and healed the sick. When they came back, Jesus took them to a quiet place to rest. Soon the crowds found out where they were and followed them. Jesus healed their sicknesses and cast out demons.

Some people even followed Jesus to the other side of the lake. The disciples said, "We'd better send these people away so they can get lunch somewhere."

Jesus said, "No. You give them something to eat."

They answered, "It would take a lot of money to buy enough food for this crowd!"

Jesus asked, "How much food do we have?"

Andrew said, "A young boy has five small loaves of bread and a couple of fish."

Jesus took the food and thanked God for it.

"Ask all the people to sit down; then pass out this food. It will be enough for everyone."

Everyone received plenty of bread and fish. So much food was left over that the disciples gathered it up in baskets so it wouldn't be wasted.

That day five thousand men plus some of their wives and children ate all they wanted!

to sink. Jesus reached out and helped him.

"Why didn't you have more faith in me?" Jesus asked. They got into the boat, and the storm stopped.

Jesus' disciples were amazed at what he had done. They said, "You really must be God's Son!"

295
Another Picnic and a Miracle

Matthew 15; Mark 7–8

Jesus healed sick people everywhere he went. Often the sick people's friends would bring them to Jesus. One day some friends brought a man who was deaf and could hardly speak. The friends begged Jesus to heal the man.

Jesus led him to a quiet place. Jesus put his fingers in the man's ears. Then he touched the man's tongue with some of his own spit.

Jesus looked up to heaven and prayed. Then he said, "Be opened!" Instantly the fellow could hear and speak perfectly.

When people realized the man was healed, they were terribly excited. Jesus asked them not to tell anyone what had happened, but they talked about it everywhere.

A huge crowd gathered, and the disciples were concerned about what the people would eat. So Jesus took a small amount of food, just seven little loaves of bread and a few fish, and made it into enough to feed everyone.

This time the crowd was made of more than four thousand people! After everyone was full, the disciples gathered up seven baskets of leftovers.

294
Jesus Walks Across the Lake

Matthew 14; Mark 6; John 6

The people said, "This man is a great prophet!" Jesus knew that they would try to make him their king, so he went up the mountain alone. The disciples waited for him, but when Jesus didn't come, the disciples decided he must have gone home another way. They got into the boat and sailed for Capernaum.

A storm came up quickly. From the shore, Jesus saw that the men were having trouble controlling their boat, so he started walking across the lake – on top of the water!

When the disciples saw him coming, they were terrified. They thought he might be a ghost! Jesus called to them and told them who he was.

Peter said, "If it's really you, let me walk on the water too."

"Come on!" Jesus said.

Peter started out bravely, but after a few steps he became afraid and started

Another said, "They think you are Elijah, come back to life. Or one of the prophets."

Jesus asked them, "But who do you say I am?"

Peter said, "You are the Christ, the Messiah."

Jesus was pleased that they understood who he was. He asked them not to tell everyone just yet. Jesus explained that the religious leaders were determined to kill him. But he promised he would rise again just three days later.

Peter said, "Oh, Lord, don't let that happen to you!"

But Jesus answered, "Don't be like Satan, the tempter. You don't understand God's plan."

296

Peter Knows Who Jesus Is

Matthew 16; Mark 8; Luke 9

Some people asked Jesus to heal a blind man. Jesus put some spit on the man's eyes and covered them with his hands. He took his hands away and asked, "Now can you see?"

The man said, "Yes. I can see people's shapes, but they look like trees walking around!"

Jesus put his hands on the man's eyes again. This time the man could see everything plainly.

As they were walking away from that town, Jesus asked his disciples, "Who do people say I am?"

"Some of them think you are John the Baptist," said one.

297

A Miracle on a Mountain

Matthew 17; Mark 9; Luke 9

Peter, James, and John were Jesus' closest friends. One day he took them up a mountain. There a remarkable thing happened to Jesus. His face and clothing shone with a bright light. Two men stood talking to Jesus about what would happen to him at the end of his life. Somehow the Lord let the disciples know that the two men were Elijah and Moses, who had been dead for hundreds of years.

Peter said, "Lord, shall we put up three tents for you and Moses and Elijah to stay in?" As Peter said this, God spoke from heaven and said, "This is my Son, whom I love. Pay attention to him and to what he says!"

The disciples were terrified at hearing

God's voice and fell to the ground. Jesus said, "You can get up. You don't need to be afraid."

When they got up, they realized that Elijah and Moses had disappeared.

Jesus said, "You must not talk about what has happened. Wait until after my death and after I come to life again." The disciples were really puzzled. What could he mean by "come to life again"?

298
Jesus Teaches About Pride

Matthew 18; Mark 9; Luke 9

One day the disciples were walking along the road. They were arguing about which one of them was going to be the greatest person in the kingdom Jesus was going to have!

Later, Jesus asked them, "What were you quarrelling about back there?"

They didn't want to talk about it, but Jesus already knew the answer because he could always tell what people were thinking and saying.

Jesus said, "Listen! If you want to be great, you must become a servant to other people. If you want to be first, you must be willing to be last."

Then he picked up and held a small child in his arms. "If you welcome a little child because of your love for me, then you are welcoming me and my Father. Don't act so proud and selfish; believe in me the way little children do. And never hurt a child. People who are cruel to children would be better off if they had never been born."

299
A Really Good Neighbour

Luke 10

One day a man asked Jesus, "Master, how can I be saved?"

Jesus answered, "You know the Law. What does it say?"

The man said, "It says to love God and my neighbour."

"Then do it," said Jesus.

"But who is my neighbour?" the lawyer asked.

Jesus said, "One day a man was travelling from Jerusalem to Jericho. Robbers attacked him. They stole his clothing and left him badly hurt.

"A priest came along, but he ignored the injured man and hurried by. Then came a Levite, or Temple worker. He didn't stop either.

"Then came a Samaritan. Samaritans don't usually like Jews. But this Samaritan took care of the man and bandaged his wounds.

"The Samaritan put the injured man on his donkey, took him to a hotel, and paid for a room where he could recover. The Samaritan told the owner he would pay more later if the money wasn't enough."

Jesus asked, "Which of the three men who saw the victim on the road acted like his neighbour?"

The lawyer said, "The one who took care of him, of course."

"That's right," Jesus answered. "Now, you do the same for others. That's the way to 'love your neighbour'."

300
Learning to Pray

Luke 10–11

Jesus had good friends in Bethany – two sisters, Mary and Martha, and their brother, Lazarus. When Jesus visited them, Martha wanted to prepare fancy meals for him. She wanted her sister to

help her, but Mary preferred to sit and listen to Jesus talk.

Martha became angry with Mary. She said to Jesus, "I wish you would tell my sister to come and help me with the cooking."

Jesus said, "Learning about God is more important than food, Martha. Mary has made a good choice."

Later Jesus taught his disciples this prayer:

"Our Father in heaven, your name is holy and should be respected by everyone. We want your kingdom to come. We want people on earth to do what you want, just as the angels in heaven do.

"Please give us the food we need today. Forgive our sins, just as we forgive the sins of people who do wrong to us. Don't let us be tempted to do evil things, but keep us away from sin. You are the glorious and powerful ruler. Amen."

301
A Blind Beggar
John 9

One day Jesus and his disciples saw a beggar who had been blind all his life. The disciples asked Jesus, "Is this man blind because he has sinned or because of his parents' sins?"

Jesus answered, "Neither. His blindness is an opportunity for God to show his glory and power."

Jesus mixed up a sort of clay by spitting on some dirt. He put it on the blind man's eyes and said, "Go and wash it off in the pool of Siloam."

The blind man obeyed. Immediately he could see.

People looked at him and said, "Isn't this the blind beggar?" Some thought he was. Others weren't sure.

The man himself said, "Yes, I am the one who was blind, but now I can see."

"How did this happen?" people asked.

The man explained what Jesus had done.

The people looked for Jesus, but they couldn't find him.

The man's friends said, "We had better take you to the Pharisee leaders to be examined.

302
Open Eyes, Open Heart
John 9

The Pharisees asked the formerly blind man how he had been healed. He told them everything Jesus had done. They said, "He did it on the Sabbath, so he can't be a very good man! Who do you think he is?"

The man said, "He is a prophet!"

The leaders still doubted the man, so they asked his parents, "Is this really your son who was blind?"

"Yes," they said. "But we don't know how our son received his sight. He can tell you." They were afraid of the Pharisees.

Jesus' enemies talked to the man again. "Give God the credit for healing you, not Jesus. He is a sinner."

The man answered, "All I know is that I was blind before, but I can see now."

The Pharisees kept questioning him. Finally the man became angry. "Why do you keep asking me about it? Do you want to believe in him too?"

Then the Pharisees scolded the man and banned him from the synagogue.

Later Jesus asked him, "Do you believe in God's Son?"

"I would if I knew who he was," the man answered.

"I am the One," Jesus said.

Then the man said, "I do believe in you!"

303
Jesus is Our Shepherd

John 9–10

Jesus said, "I have come to make blind people see – and to make some people who think they can see realize how blind they are!" The Pharisees asked if he was speaking about them. Jesus answered, "If you knew you were blind, you would not be sinful; but because you think you have such good eyes, you are guilty of sin!" Then Jesus said, "If a person climbs over a fence into the sheep pen, we know he is a thief. The

one who enters through the door is the real shepherd. His sheep know him. "I am like a good shepherd to those who love me. I am willing to sacrifice my life for my sheep. I know my sheep, and they know me."

Then Jesus talked about God, his Father. "My Father loves me because I will give up my life and will get it back again."

The Pharisees were shocked and angry when Jesus said God was his Father. They even thought an evil spirit was controlling him.

But people who had seen his miracles said, "Look at the good things he does for people! How could he heal a blind man if he had a demon?"

304
Jesus' Good Friend Dies

John 11

One day Lazarus became very sick. His sisters, Mary and Martha, were afraid he might die, so they sent word to Jesus, asking him to come and heal Lazarus. Jesus didn't rush to Bethany at once. He said, "The purpose of this illness is not Lazarus's death; it is intended to bring glory to me, the Son of God." And he stayed away from Bethany for two more days.

At last he said, "Let's go to Bethany now. Lazarus has gone to sleep, and I must wake him up."

At first his disciples didn't understand, but then he said, "Lazarus is dead, and when you see what I will do, you will believe in me."

Martha ran out to meet Jesus. She said, "Master, if you had been here,

Lazarus wouldn't have died. But even now he would come back to life if you tell him to."

305
New Life for Lazarus

John 11

Jesus said, "Yes, your brother will rise again. I am the Resurrection and the Life. Anyone who believes in me shall rise from the dead and live forever. Do you believe this?"

Martha said, "Yes, Master. I believe you are the Messiah."

Martha went home and told Mary that Jesus wanted to talk to her. Everyone thought Mary was going to her brother's grave, so they followed her.

Mary said to Jesus, "If you had come sooner, our brother would not have died."

When Jesus saw her crying, he felt very sad, and he cried too. He asked them to take him to the grave. It was a cave in the side of a hill, with a big stone in front to seal it shut.

Jesus said, "Roll the stone away."

Martha said, "But he's been dead for four days, and his body will have decayed."

Jesus answered, "I told you I would do a miracle." Then he prayed and called out loudly to Lazarus to come out of the grave! How surprised and frightened all the people were when Lazarus appeared!

Jesus said, "Unwrap those tightly bound cloths, and let him go!" Then Lazarus went home with his sisters.

306
Ten Are Healed; One is Grateful

Luke 17

One day Jesus said to the disciples, "If a friend commits a sin, tell him it is wrong. If he is sorry, be sure to forgive him. Even if he does it again and again, you must be willing to keep on forgiving him."

Another time ten men who had leprosy came to meet Jesus. They couldn't come too close because everyone thought leprosy was contagious. They called out to Jesus, "Master, please take pity on us." Jesus cared about sick and hurting people. He said, "Go and show yourselves to the priest." By law lepers had to do this when they thought their disease was cured. The priest had to agree they were well before they could go home and live normally.

As the ten men walked toward the Temple, their skin became clear and healthy! One of the ten, a Samaritan, hurried back to Jesus, fell down at his feet, and cried out with joy, "Praise God! I'm completely healed!"

Jesus said, "Didn't I heal ten men? Where are the other nine? You are the only one to come back and give thanks. Because you have faith, you have been healed."

— 307 —
Healing on the Sabbath
Luke 13

This story is about a woman whose back had been crippled for eighteen years so she could not stand upright. One Sabbath day she went to her local synagogue, and Jesus was there to teach. He saw her stiff, bent back, and he felt sad about her pain.

Jesus said to her, "Woman, your back is completely healed."

As soon as he had said these words and touched her, she was able to stand up straight like everyone else! She was so happy that she praised God and thanked him.

The synagogue leader was angry because Jesus had healed someone on the Sabbath day. The leader yelled, "You have plenty of other days to heal people. You don't need to break the Sabbath!"

Jesus answered, "You take your animals from their stalls and lead them out to get water on the Sabbath day, don't you? If you do that for a mere animal, shouldn't I do a kindness for this human being – a daughter of Abraham – who has been in this terrible condition for eighteen years?"

These words made his enemies feel ashamed of themselves. And the crowds of people were happy because of this miracle Jesus had done.

— 308 —
Looking for the Lost
Luke 15

One day some Pharisees were grumbling about the bad people Jesus spent time with. Jesus heard them and said, "Suppose you were a shepherd with a hundred sheep to care for. If one of them wandered away from the flock, what would you do? Wouldn't you leave the other ninety-nine sheep in the sheep pen and go out to hunt for the lost one until you found it? Then you would carry it home and celebrate with your friends and neighbours. I, too, am more concerned about the one who is lost than I am about the ninety-nine who do not stray." Then he said, "If a woman has ten coins and she loses one in her home, don't you think she will look in every corner and crack and sweep the floor carefully until she finds it? Then she will be happy because she has found her valuable coin. She will call in her friends to celebrate with her. And so the angels in heaven are happy when one sinner repents and is found by God."

309
The Son Who Ran Away

Luke 15

Jesus told another story, this time about a farmer's younger son. The son was tired of helping on his father's farm, so he said, "Father, give me my share of your money so I can leave home."

The father divided his property between his two sons. The younger one took his share, packed up his clothes, and went far away from home.

He made lots of friends because he had plenty of money. But after he had carelessly wasted everything, his "friends" disappeared.

The only job he could find was tending pigs. No Jewish boy liked pigs because they were unclean. But it was the best he could do. He was so hungry he could have eaten the dry husks of the pigs' food.

He began thinking how comfortable his home had been and decided he would go back and confess to his father that he had done the wrong thing and didn't deserve to be his son anymore. Then maybe his father would let him become one of the servants.

His father hoped that his son would return home. When, one day, the father saw his son walking down the road toward him, he ran up to him, then hugged and kissed him!

310
The Runaway Returns

Luke 15

The runaway son began to explain: "Father, I have sinned against you…"

But before the son could ask if he could become a servant, his father called to one of his slaves, "Bring my son some good clothes, some decent shoes, and a ring for his finger. Kill that fat calf in the pen, and we'll have a feast to celebrate."

When the older son had finished working in the fields, he came home to hear the sound of music and fun. When he realized the party was in honour of his younger brother, he wasn't very happy.

The older son said to his father, "I've always been a good son and a hard worker, but nobody ever gave me a big party! My brother has been out wasting your hard-earned money, and when he comes home broke, you invite friends round for a celebration. You've even killed the best calf!"

His father said, "Don't be angry. You are my dear son, and everything I have is yours. But we should be happy because my son who was lost is found."

311
The Rich Man and the Beggar

Luke 16

The Pharisees were very proud, and they loved being rich. One day Jesus told them this story: "A rich man lived in a large, expensive home. He had beautiful clothes and everything else he wanted. At his gate lay a poor dirty beggar, begging money from passers-by. His name was Lazarus. He was covered with sores, and he didn't have proper food.

"Lazarus died. Angels took him to heaven, so he was with Abraham. Then the rich man died too, but he went to the place of fiery torment called hell. The rich man could see up into heaven, where Lazarus was now happy and comfortable.

"The rich man called to Abraham, 'Please send Lazarus down here to relieve my suffering.'

"Abraham answered, 'You had every comfort when you were on earth. Poor Lazarus had nothing. Now it is the other way around.'

"The rich man cried out, 'Please send Lazarus back to warn my brothers so they can escape this place.'

"But Abraham said, 'They have the Scriptures to warn them. If they won't believe them, they won't believe someone who comes back from the dead.'"

— 312 —
Jesus Loves Little Children

Matthew 19; Mark 10; Luke 18

Jesus loved children. One day while he was teaching the people, some mothers brought their children up close to Jesus because they wanted him to give the children a special blessing.

The disciples thought they shouldn't interrupt Jesus while he was talking, so they scolded the women and tried to get them to leave.

Jesus stopped the disciples at once. "Don't send them away. Don't prevent children from coming to me. They are the very ones for whom my kingdom is

intended. Everyone who wants to be in my kingdom should be like these little children – pure and trusting and loving."

Then he picked the children up and held them in his arms. He often warned people never to do any harm to a child. Children are important to Jesus, and he loves them very much.

313

Jesus Heals Bartimaeus' Eyes

Matthew 20; Mark 10; Luke 18

A blind man named Bartimaeus lived near Jericho. One day he heard that Jesus was coming, and he knew that Jesus often healed people with serious problems like his. Bartimaeus couldn't see Jesus, of course, but he sat by the side of the road and called out, "Jesus, Son of David, please have mercy on me! O Son of David, have pity on me!"

Some of the people around him became cross. "Oh, do be quiet!" they growled.

He called out all the louder, "Please, Jesus, help me!"

When Jesus finally heard him, he said, "Tell that man I want to talk to him."

"Come on, Bartimaeus," the people said. "Jesus wants to see you."

Jesus asked Bartimaeus, "What do you want me to do for you?"

Bartimaeus replied eagerly, "Oh, Teacher, I want you to give me my sight!"

"All right," said Jesus, "it's done. Your faith has healed you." From that moment Bartimaeus was able to see perfectly!

314

The Man in the Tree

Luke 19

Another man in Jericho was eager to see Jesus. Zacchaeus collected taxes for the Roman government. The people hated the Romans, so they disliked Jews who worked for the Romans. Tax collectors were especially hated because most of them were dishonest.

Zacchaeus was very short. He was so determined to see Jesus that he climbed into a sycamore tree. When Jesus and his disciples came near to the tree, Jesus looked up and spoke directly to the little man: "Zacchaeus, come down; I am going to your home today."

Some people in the crowd were shocked. "Look! He's going to the home of a terrible sinner!" they muttered.

Zacchaeus welcomed Jesus gladly. He said, "Master, I want to give half of my money to the poor. And since I got some of my riches by cheating the taxpayers, I will give back four times as much as I stole."

Jesus could see that Zacchaeus' faith had changed his heart. Jesus said, "I came to look for lost people and save them. Today salvation has come to this house."

315
Crowds Welcome Jesus to Jerusalem

Matthew 21; Mark 11; Luke 19; John 12

Jesus decided to go to Jerusalem. First he stopped in Bethany to visit Martha, Mary, and Lazarus. Then he sent two of his disciples to a nearby town to find a donkey's colt on which he could ride into the city. They brought the animal and put their coats on it to make it more comfortable for Jesus.

As he rode into Jerusalem, great crowds of people gathered to welcome him. They put their coats and branches of palm trees down on the road. They shouted their welcome to him: "God bless the Son of David! He comes in the name of the Lord!"

Jesus went into the Temple. When he saw merchants and moneychangers cheating the people, he shouted, "My Temple should be a place of prayer, but you have turned it into a robbers' den!" And Jesus drove them out of the Temple.

Jesus healed sick people in the Temple. Children called out, "God bless David's Son!" The leaders were angry and asked Jesus if he heard what they were saying.

"Yes," he said. "The eighth psalm says that babies and children shall praise the Lord!"

— 316 —
The Farmer's Son
Matthew 21; Mark 12; Luke 20

Jesus taught in the Temple every day. This is one of his story lessons: "Once a rich farmer had a large vineyard. He rented it out and left town. At harvest time he sent a man to get his share of the grapes. But the renter beat the man up and wouldn't give him anything.

"The owner sent another helper, but the same thing happened. The owner even sent a third one, but he, too, was beaten and chased away.

"Then the owner thought, 'If I send my own son, surely they will respect him, and I'll get my share of the crop.' But when his son got there, the tenant farmers said, 'He will inherit the farm. If we kill him, we can keep the land.' So they attacked and killed the son."

Then Jesus asked, "What do you think the owner will do then? He will come and kill those wicked renters and find new people to take care of his farm." The Temple leaders realized they were the tenant farmers of Jesus' story and Jesus was the owner's Son, whom they were planning to kill. They wanted to arrest him, but he was so popular with the people that they didn't dare.

317
Clothes for a Wedding
Matthew 22

Jesus knew he would not be with his followers much longer. He wanted them to be ready to get along without him. He told them this story lesson: "A king's son was about to be married. He invited many friends to the wedding feast, but when the time came, they didn't show up. The king sent servants out to bring them to the feast.

"Some refused to come because they were too busy. Some were cruel to the servants and killed them.

"The king sent more servants out to invite a new group of people to the wedding: 'Bring everyone you can find on the street or anywhere else.'

"As each guest came, the king gave him or her new clothes to wear at the wedding feast. When the room was full, he greeted his guests. He noticed one man who was not wearing the special wedding clothing. The king said, 'How did you get in here without the proper clothing?'

"The man had no answer, so the king ordered the servants to tie up his hands and feet and throw him out into the darkness.

"The king said, 'I called many, but I chose only a few.'"

318
Oil for the Lamps

Matthew 25

Jesus said that getting ready for his kingdom would be like a group of ten bridesmaids preparing to welcome home a bridegroom and his bride after a wedding. Five of the bridesmaids brought extra oil so they could refill and relight their lamps when they heard the bridegroom coming. The other five girls didn't bother.

The bridegroom was late, so the girls went to sleep. Then someone shouted, "He's coming! Quick! Get up and light your lamps!" But five of them didn't have any more oil, so they couldn't light their lamps.

They asked the other five girls for some of their extra oil. But they said, "We have used it all. You will have to go out and buy some." While they were gone, the bridegroom came, and the wedding feast began.

When the five girls returned, they knocked loudly on the locked door and asked permission to come in. But the bridegroom didn't let them come in.

319
Using Our Talents

Matthew 25

Here's another story about living wisely. A rich boss gave his employees money to invest while he was away. He gave five thousand coins to one, two thousand coins to another, and one thousand to the third.

The first man doubled his money. The second man used his money wisely too, and he had extra money as a result. The third man just hid his thousand coins, so it wouldn't get lost or stolen.

When the employer came back, he asked each man how he had used the money. The first man showed his boss the large profit he had made. The employer was very pleased and gave the employee a big reward.

The second fellow did the same. Again the boss was pleased, and he rewarded that employee too.

When the third man came, he was embarrassed, but he said, "I knew you would demand a report, so I was careful not to lose your money. I kept it safe in a hidden place." The employer was disappointed, and he took back his thousand coins. He punished the employee for not using the money more wisely.

320
The Sheep and the Goats
Matthew 25

One day Jesus told his disciples how he would choose the people for his kingdom. Jesus said, "I'll come back to the earth in great glory, and everyone will stand before my throne. I will be like a shepherd separating the sheep from the goats.

"Then I'll say to the 'sheep', 'Come into my kingdom. I want you because when I was hungry, you fed me. When I was thirsty, you gave me something to drink. When I was a stranger, you invited me into your homes. And when I was sick or in prison, you visited me.'

"They will answer, 'Lord, we don't remember doing those things for you.'

"And I will say, 'When you cared for needy people, it was just as if you were caring for me.' Then I will say to the 'goats', 'You must be thrown into the everlasting fire because when poor people needed help, you neglected them, and so you were really neglecting me.'"

321
A Gift of Love
Matthew 26; Mark 14; John 12

One evening Jesus' friends in Bethany had a dinner for him. Martha served the meal, as usual. The guests leaned back on couches around the table. Mary entered the room carrying a large jar of very expensive perfume. She knelt in front of Jesus. She broke the jar and poured the perfume over his feet. Then she dried them, not with a towel, but with her long hair.

Judas Iscariot was the treasurer of the group of disciples. He was always thinking about money. He was shocked at what Mary had done, and he said, "Master! A big jar of perfume like that could have been sold and the money used to take care of a lot of poor people."

Jesus knew what was in Judas's heart and said, "Don't complain about what Mary has done. She has shown her love for me in a beautiful way, and the world will never forget what she has done.

"You will always have poor people to take care of, but I won't always be here. This woman has anointed me in advance for my burial!"

322
The Disciples Celebrate Passover
Matthew 26; Mark 14; Luke 22

The disciples asked Jesus where they should prepare the Passover feast. Jesus said, "Walk to the edge of the city, and you will see a man carrying a pitcher of water. Follow that man to his house. Then say to him, 'Please show us the room you have prepared for the Master.' He will show you a room that is all ready for Passover."

They did as Jesus told them, and later in the day Jesus and more of his followers came for the Passover dinner.

Jesus said, "This is the last Passover

I will celebrate before I am sacrificed for the world's sins."

The disciples couldn't understand this. They had always supposed Jesus would become the powerful king who would free them from the Roman government. They even started arguing about who was going to be the most important one in Jesus' kingdom. Jesus said to them, "Anyone who wants to be the most important must become unimportant. The way to be a leader is to be a servant!"

323

Jesus Washes the Disciples' Feet

John 13

Jesus showed the disciples exactly what he meant when he said a leader must be a servant. He asked them, "Who is greater, the master or the servant?" Of course they said, "The master!"

Jesus said, "Well, I am the master of this feast, but I am also your servant."

Then he took a basin of water,

stooped down, and washed the disciples' feet and dried them with a towel.

Peter said, "Lord, I don't want you to wash my feet!"

Jesus answered, "If I don't, you won't really belong to me."

"Then wash every part of me!" Peter said.

"That isn't necessary, Peter," Jesus said. "If I have washed your feet, you are clean all over. But that isn't true of everyone in this room." He knew that one of the disciples was going to betray him.

Jesus said, "Do you understand what I just did? If I, the Master, have washed your feet, how much more important it is that you wash one another's feet. I've given you a good example; now follow it."

324
The Last Supper

Matthew 26; Mark 14; Luke 22; John 13

John asked Jesus what he meant when he said one of them was not loyal. Jesus said, "It will be the one to whom I give this piece of bread after I dip it into the bowl." He handed the bread to Judas Iscariot and said, "Go and do what you have to do."

Then Satan made Judas even more determined to betray Jesus. Judas left and went out into the night.

Jesus said, "I won't be with you much longer. I want to give you a new commandment. You must love one another as I have loved you! It will show the world that you belong to me."

Then Jesus took a piece of bread and broke it. "This is my body, which will be broken for you. When you eat this bread, you will show my death to everyone."

Next he took a cup of wine and blessed it. "This wine is my blood, poured out for you so God will forgive your sins. Drink this in memory of me."

Jesus said his followers should do this over and over until he returns to earth again.

325
Jesus Prays in the Garden

Matthew 26; Mark 14; Luke 22; John 13–14

Peter said, "I love you so much that I would even die for you!"

Jesus shook his head sadly. "Peter. Before the rooster crows tomorrow morning, you'll say three times that you don't even know me!"

Jesus promised that while he was gone the Holy Spirit would live in them and comfort them. Then they went to the Garden of Gethsemane for prayer. Jesus took Peter, James, and John with him to a private place. He said, "Wait here and pray."

As Jesus prayed alone, he thought about how terrible his death would be. He prayed for a while, then went back and found the disciples sleeping. Jesus said, "Can't you stay awake and pray for me?"

He went back to pray some more. His heart was in such pain that he sweated drops of blood. Jesus cried out, "Father, if it is possible, keep me from this death. However, I want to do your will, not my own."

He returned to the disciples and again he found them asleep. This time he just said, "Go on sleeping. You need your rest."

326
Soldiers Arrest Jesus

Matthew 26; Mark 14; Luke 22; John 18

Jesus prayed a while longer; then he went back to Peter, James, and John. He said, "Get up now. Judas is coming to betray me." They all jumped up and saw a group of soldiers and Temple officials coming through the garden. The soldiers had lanterns and torches and were carrying weapons.

Jesus knew what was going to happen, but he asked, "What do you want?"

They answered, "We've come for Jesus of Nazareth."

He said, "I am the one you want."

Peter was so angry with Jesus' enemies that he grabbed his sword and cut off the ear of the high priest's servant, Malchus.

Jesus said, "Put your sword away, Peter. Shouldn't I do whatever the Father requires?" Then Jesus healed Malchus's ear.

Jesus said, "You come after me as if I were a robber. Why didn't you arrest me when I was teaching in the Temple?"

The soldiers arrested Jesus and took him to the high priest.

327

Peter Hears the Rooster Crow

Matthew 26; Mark 14; Luke 22; John 18

As the soldiers took Jesus away, Peter followed. While Jesus was being questioned inside the house, Peter waited in the courtyard. A servant girl looked at Peter. She said, "I think I've seen that man with Jesus."

Peter was afraid, so he said, "No! I don't even know him."

Later another person looked at him closely and said, "Yes, this man is a disciple of the man from Nazareth."

But again Peter said, "I certainly am not!"

A third person said, "He must be one of Jesus' people. He talks like a Galilean."

Peter was more frightened than ever, and he shouted, "You don't know what you are talking about! I've had nothing to do with that man Jesus."

As he said those words, Jesus was being led across the courtyard. Jesus turned and looked at Peter, and then a rooster crowed!

Immediately Peter remembered that Jesus had said Peter would deny that he knew him three times before the rooster crowed. Peter cried because he was ashamed that he had been so unfaithful to the Master he loved.

328
Officials Question Jesus

Matthew 26; Mark 14; Luke 22; John 18

Members of the Jewish high court questioned Jesus and other people about Jesus' teachings. Many people lied about him, trying to get him into trouble. The high priest asked if he was the Son of God. Jesus answered, "Yes, I am. And one day you will see me sitting beside God the Father in heaven."

The court was shocked. The high priest yelled, "He claims to be God's Son! What shall we do with him?"

Everyone thought Jesus should be killed. They made fun of him, spat on him, and hit him.

They led him to the Roman governor, Pontius Pilate. They lied, saying Jesus had tried to get Jews to rebel against the Roman government. "He even says he is the king of the Jews," they said.

Pilate asked Jesus, "Is that true? Are you a king?"

Jesus answered, "Yes, I am, but not in the way you mean. I have a kingdom, but it is not on earth."

Pilate said to the Jewish court officials, "He doesn't seem to have done anything wrong."

But the officials and the people made such an uproar about it that Pilate decided to send Jesus to be questioned by Herod.

329
Pilate Frees One Prisoner

Matthew 27; Mark 15; Luke 23; John 18–19

Herod talked to Jesus, but Jesus wouldn't answer. Finally Herod gave up. He and his soldiers mocked Jesus and mistreated him, then sent him back to Pilate. Pilate said, "This man hasn't done anything bad enough to die for."

Each year Pilate had the privilege of setting one Jewish prisoner free at the time of the Passover. He asked the crowds which prisoner he should set free that year – Jesus or a murderer named Barabbas. The crowds shouted, "Barabbas! Set Barabbas free!"

Pilate asked, "If I free Barabbas, what shall I do with Jesus?"

Everyone screamed, "Crucify him! Crucify him!"

Pilate's wife sent him a message that said, "Don't condemn Jesus. I had a dream about him last night, and I know he is innocent!"

But Pilate thought he had to give the people what they wanted. He called for a bowl of water and washed his

hands in front of them. "All right. Take him and crucify him. I wash my hands of responsibility. Don't blame me for Jesus' death."

330
A Crown of Thorns

Matthew 27; Mark 15; John 19

Pilate's soldiers mocked Jesus. They made a crown of thorns, and they pushed it onto Jesus' head. Pilate hoped he could get the religious leaders to leave Jesus alone. He said again. "He really doesn't deserve to die."

But the leaders said, "If you don't let us crucify him, we'll tell the emperor that you let one of his enemies escape!"

So Pilate stopped objecting and said, "You may crucify him. But I don't think he is guilty!"

Judas, who had betrayed Jesus, was sorry for what he had done. Judas took back the thirty pieces of silver the religious leaders had paid him.

He said, "I don't want your money. I did the wrong thing when I betrayed the Lord."

The religious leaders just laughed at him and said, "That's too bad! It's too late now!"

Judas was so sad about turning against Jesus that he took his own life by hanging himself.

— 331 —
The Crucifixion

Matthew 27; Mark 15; Luke 23; John 19

The soldiers made Jesus carry the heavy wooden cross up a hill called Calvary. Jesus stumbled under the heavy weight. Then the soldiers got a man from the crowd to carry it for him.

Jesus lay down on the cross. They hammered nails through his hands and feet and stood the cross upright.

There Jesus hung, in great pain, for several hours.

He prayed that his heavenly Father would forgive his enemies. "They don't understand what they are doing," Jesus said.

The soldiers divided up his clothes. They rolled dice to see who would get his robe.

Pilate had told them to put a sign on the cross over Jesus' head saying "Jesus of Nazareth, the King of the Jews."

Two criminals were crucified at the same time as Jesus, and one of them believed in Jesus. The criminal said, "Please remember me when you have your kingdom."

Jesus answered, "This very day you will be with me in heaven!"

332
Jesus Dies on the Cross

Matthew 27; Mark 15; Luke 23; John 19

Jesus' family and friends stood near the cross. His mother, Mary, and the other women who were his followers were there, as well as the eleven disciples. Jesus said to the disciple John, "John, treat Mary as if she were your own mother." And he said to Mary, "John is to be like your son."

Jesus suffered most because he was dying as a sinner even though he had never done anything wrong. He did it to accept the punishment that should have been ours.

Jesus was very lonely as he died. He cried out, "O my God, why have you left me?"

The sky turned dark, even though it was early afternoon. Jesus said he was thirsty, and someone gave him a taste of sour wine.

Then he cried out loudly, "It is finished!" And he died. At that moment an earthquake shook the ground. The curtain in front of the Most Holy Place in the Temple was torn from top to bottom.

One of the Roman soldiers near the cross said in amazement, "Why, this man really was God's Son!"

333
Jesus is Buried

Matthew 27; Mark 15; Luke 23; John 19

One day after the crucifixion was the Sabbath, so the religious leaders wanted Jesus' body removed from the cross before the Sabbath began. The religious leaders said, "Be sure all the men you crucified are really dead; then take them down."

When the soldiers looked at Jesus, they saw that he was already dead.

A man named Joseph of Arimathea had admired Jesus very much. He had kept it a secret because he was a member of the Jewish religious council and the rest of the members were Jesus' enemies.

Joseph owned a burial cave in a garden not far from where Jesus was crucified. He asked Pilate for permission to bury Jesus' body in his tomb.

Joseph took Jesus' body, wrapped it in a linen cloth, and laid it in his tomb. Jesus' mother and the other women watched as Joseph rolled a heavy stone in front of the tomb; then they went away, feeling very sad and lonely.

334
Alive Again!

Matthew 28; Mark 16; Luke 24; John 20

Jesus' enemies asked Pilate to put guards by Jesus' tomb. "His disciples might come and steal his body and then pretend he has risen from the dead," they said. The women wanted to prepare Jesus' body for burial, but they couldn't do it until the Sabbath was over. Very early in the morning, on the day after the Sabbath, the women went to the tomb carrying the necessary spices.

When they got there, they were surprised to see that the stone was already rolled away from the tomb. They looked in and saw an angel sitting where Jesus' body had been!

The women were afraid, but the angel said, "Don't be afraid. Jesus is not here. He has come to life. Tell his disciples he is alive and will meet them in Galilee."

As the women hurried away, they saw Jesus in the garden. "Don't hold on to me. Go and tell my disciples that I'm alive and will see them in Galilee," he said.

When the women told the disciples, they could hardly believe it. Peter and John hurried to the tomb to see for themselves, and they found that the tomb was indeed empty!

335
The Disciples See Jesus Alive

Mark 16; Luke 24; John 20

The disciples could hardly believe that Jesus had actually come to life. But soon they began to see proof. Two disciples were walking to Emmaus. They were still very sad about Jesus' death. Suddenly Jesus was there with them, but they didn't recognize him.

Jesus asked them why they were so sad, and they said, "Don't you know what happened to Jesus last week? His enemies crucified him! Some of our people heard that he has risen, but how can we tell?"

Jesus talked to them for a long time, explaining all the Scriptures that told about the Saviour and how they applied to him. The disciples invited him to supper, and when Jesus broke bread

they realized they had been talking with Jesus all that time!

He disappeared, but they hurried back to Jerusalem to tell everyone that Jesus was alive.

They learned that Peter had seen Jesus too. While they were talking about him, Jesus appeared to all of them! He showed them the nail wounds in his hands and feet; then he ate some supper with them.

336
The Disciples Go Fishing

John 21

One day Peter and several other disciples went fishing. They fished all night but didn't catch anything. Toward morning they saw a man on the shore. They didn't recognize him as Jesus. He called to them, "How's the fishing?"

They answered, "We haven't caught anything!"

He said, "Throw the nets on the other side of the boat."

They did, and immediately the nets were so full of fish the men couldn't pull them aboard.

John shouted, "It must be our Lord!"

Peter swam ashore – he was so happy to see Jesus. The men dragged the net in. They had caught about 150 fish.

Jesus was cooking some fish over a small fire on the shore. After breakfast he talked to Peter alone. He asked Peter if he really loved him. Peter said he did, so Jesus said, "Then you must spend your life feeding my sheep and my lambs."

He meant that Peter must tell others

about what Jesus had done for them and show them how to live as faithful followers of the Lord.

337
Back to Heaven

Matthew 28; Mark 16; Luke 24; Acts 1

One day Jesus went up on a mountain with a group of his followers. He said, "God has given me all power and authority. Go and preach to people all over the world. Teach them to obey the rules and advice I have given you. When they believe in me, baptize them in the name of the Father, the Son, and the Holy Spirit. I will always be with you, to the end of the world."

Jesus told his disciples to stay in Jerusalem. In a few days the Holy Spirit would come to them and give them special power to do the things Jesus had told them.

Then he led the group toward

Bethany. Jesus gave his blessing to all his friends. Then he went up into the sky until he disappeared into the clouds.

They saw an angel who said, "Why are you staring at the sky? Jesus has just gone to heaven, but one day he is going to return again!"

So the disciples waited for God to send the Holy Spirit as Jesus had promised.

338
The Holy Spirit Comes

Acts 2

Because Judas was gone, the disciples needed someone to take his place in the inner group of twelve. They made the choice by casting lots. Matthias was the one chosen to be the new disciple.

After about seven weeks, the disciples were still meeting regularly

and waiting for the Spirit. One day they heard a loud noise, like the roaring of a storm. Then they saw little flames of fire over their heads, and they were all filled with the Holy Spirit.

They began to speak in languages they had never known before. People who gathered to see what was happening were amazed. Most of them thought it was wonderful, but a few laughed and said, "They've been drinking!"

Peter told the crowd. "We aren't drunk! What has happened to us is exactly what the prophet Joel predicted."

Then Peter preached about how Jesus had died and risen again to take away the world's sin. About three thousand people believed his message and were baptized – and that was the start of the Christian church.

339
Obeying God, Not Men

Acts 3–4

A man in Jerusalem had been disabled all of his life. Each day his friends carried him to the gate of the Temple where he begged for money. Peter and John went to the Temple to pray. The beggar asked them for money. Peter said, "I don't have any money, but I can give you something better. In the name of Jesus, get up and walk!"

Right away the man not only walked, but he jumped around, shouting praises to God. Everyone who saw this was amazed.

Peter told them, "Jesus gave us power to do miracles. We want all of you to become his followers!"

The religious leaders arrested Peter and John and put them into prison for preaching about Jesus. After the leaders questioned the disciples (now called apostles), they had to release them because healing the man was not illegal.

But they told Peter and John, "You must not preach anymore about this Jesus of Nazareth."

Peter and John wouldn't promise that. They said, "Jesus told us to preach, and you say not to. Should we obey God or men?"

The leaders had no answer to that question!

340

Lying to God

Acts 4–5

The believers went on telling people about Jesus. They met together for prayer and worship. They loved one another and shared what they had with poor people. Sometimes they even sold their property and put the money into a fund that everyone could use.

One day Ananias brought in some money and said, "I sold my house, and I am giving the money to the treasury." But he had really sold the house for much more money and was only pretending to share it all. God told Peter what was going on.

Peter asked Ananias, "Is this all the money you got for your house?"

Ananias lied, "Yes, that's all."

Peter said, "Why do you lie? The money was yours, but you tried to deceive us." Immediately Ananias fell down dead. The men took him out for burial.

Soon his wife, Sapphira, came in. Peter said, "Sapphira, did Ananias bring all the money from the sale of your house?"

"Yes," she replied, for she and her husband had agreed to lie.

"Why do you try to fool God?" She fell dead, too, and they buried her next to Ananias.

341

The Cost of Obedience

Acts 5

The Jewish religious leaders had warned Peter and John not to preach about Jesus, but Peter and John went on doing it. The Holy Spirit came and gave them courage. They healed the sick and cast out evil spirits.

The high priest and other leaders saw that the apostles were becoming more and more popular among the people. So the leaders arrested the apostles again and put them back into prison.

But that same night an angel came and opened the prison door and let them out. They went back and taught in the Temple.

When the officials sent for the apostles to accuse them, they were gone! Someone reported that they were in the Temple, preaching, so once again they were arrested and brought before the religious council.

"Didn't we tell you to stop preaching?" said the high priest.

"Yes, but we must obey our Lord and tell everyone about him."

Their enemies were really furious with them. But a wise man, Gamaliel, said, "Let's be patient and find out whether these men are telling the truth. If after a while they disappear and nothing comes of their preaching, we'll know they were wrong."

342
A Good Man Dies for His Faith

Acts 6–7

As the group of believers grew, the apostles became very busy. They chose seven helpers to look after the money and feed the poor. One of the helpers was Stephen. His preaching made the believers' enemies angry, so they found an excuse to arrest him. The religious leaders asked him about Jesus, and Stephen preached a long message. He reminded them of everything God had done for his people. Stephen said Jesus was the one who had come to fulfil the promises the prophets had made many years ago.

Then he accused the leaders of killing Jesus and rejecting the Good News. The religious leaders shouted terrible things at him, but Stephen looked up into the sky and said, "I see the Son of God at his Father's right hand in heaven!"

They dragged him out of the city. They took off their robes. A young man named Saul guarded their clothing as they threw heavy, sharp stones at Stephen. He was so badly hurt that he died.

As Stephen was dying, he prayed, "Lord, don't blame them for this sin!"

343
Saul is Cruel to Christians

Acts 8

Stephen's death was the beginning of a new wave of cruelty against the believers in Jerusalem. Saul was one of the worst enemies of the church. All the believers were afraid of him.

The believers spoke about Jesus wherever they went. Philip went into Samaria, where he preached and healed people.

One day as Philip was travelling, he saw a man from Ethiopia riding in a chariot. The man was reading something, and he looked troubled. He had been reading Isaiah's prophecies about Jesus and couldn't understand them. Philip explained what Isaiah meant, and he told the Ethiopian all about Jesus.

The man asked if he could be baptized.

"Yes," said Philip, "if you truly believe."

"I do believe that Jesus is the Son of God," the Ethiopian answered. So Philip baptized him in a nearby stream.

344
Saul Sees the Light!

Acts 9

Saul decided to go to Damascus and find believers to arrest. He took some soldiers with him. As he travelled, something very strange happened.

A brilliant light shone down out of heaven, and a voice said, "Saul, I am Jesus. Why are you trying to hurt me?"

"What should I do, Lord?" Saul asked.

"Go to Damascus and wait for instructions," the voice said.

The soldiers heard the voice but didn't see anyone. When the light and the voice were gone, Saul realized he was blind.

Then the Lord spoke to Ananias, a disciple in Damascus. "Go to Judas's home, in Straight Street. Ask for Saul of Tarsus. I've told him you will come and give him back his sight."

"O Lord, I'm afraid! Saul is a terrible enemy of all believers."

was the Messiah, God's Son. They decided to kill him. They watched the city gate, planning to capture him if he tried to leave. But the believers heard about the plot and helped Saul escape. They let him down over the city wall in a big basket!

Saul returned to Jerusalem and tried to join the believers' fellowship. But they were afraid of him. One of their members, Barnabas, knew what had happened on the road to Damascus. He took Saul to the believers and said,

"Don't worry. I've chosen him to be my messenger not only to Jews but to Gentiles, too!"

Ananias obeyed. He found Saul and said, "The Lord has sent me so you can receive your sight and be filled with the Holy Spirit."

And that is what happened! From then on Saul was a faithful follower of the Lord Jesus.

345
Can the Believers Trust Saul?

Acts 9

The news quickly spread among the Christians that their old enemy Saul was now saying he believed in Jesus. He was even preaching the gospel in Damascus. Some were glad to hear this, but others didn't trust him.

Some Jews in Damascus became angry with Saul because he said Jesus

"Listen! You know I would not trick you. Let me tell you how Saul became a believer." Then he told them the whole story.

"He really is one of us," Barnabas said. From then on, the church accepted Saul.

346
Peter Sees a Vision

Acts 9–10

Dorcas was a believer in Joppa who did kind things for poor people. When she died, her friends asked Peter to come quickly. Peter asked them to leave the room. He prayed; then he said, "Dorcas, get up!" She came back to life and joined her friends.

Cornelius was a Roman army officer in Caesarea. One night an angel appeared to him and said, "God knows that you want to understand more about him. Send messengers to Joppa to find Simon Peter. Invite him to visit you."

Cornelius obeyed. Meanwhile, in Joppa, Peter also had a vision. He was praying on the roof of the house where he was staying. It was lunchtime, and Peter was hungry. Suddenly he saw a sheet coming down from the sky. On it were many kinds of animals, including some the Jews weren't allowed to eat.

A voice said, "Kill and eat whatever you want."

Peter said, "No! I would never eat unclean things."

The voice replied, "If God says the food is all right, believe him!"

The same thing

happened three times. Peter wondered what this strange vision could possibly mean.

347
A Gentile Believer

Acts 10

While Peter was trying to understand his strange vision, Cornelius's messengers arrived. Peter met the messengers. They told him all about Cornelius and his vision.

Peter invited them in, and the next morning they left for Caesarea. When they arrived, Cornelius welcomed them into his home, where he had gathered friends and relatives. Cornelius fell down and worshipped Peter.

"Don't do that! I'm not a god," said Peter.

Peter said, "Jews don't usually go into the homes of non-Jews. But God gave me a vision, and now I

understand it. It means I should never think of other people as unclean or worthless. God told me to come, and here I am. How can I help you?"

Cornelius told him that he wanted to be a believer, so Peter taught him about Jesus. He said, "Anyone who believes in Jesus will have his sins forgiven."

Cornelius and his family believed, and when Peter saw that they were true believers, he baptized all of them.

348
An Angel Sets Peter Free

Acts 12

King Herod began to get tough with the believers. He killed John's brother James and put Peter in jail, planning to kill him, too. All the believers prayed very hard for Peter.

The night before he was to be killed, Peter was sleeping in the prison. He was chained to two soldiers. An angel came and woke Peter.

The angel said, "Get up quickly, dress, and follow me." The chains fell off Peter's arms, and he followed the angel.

The angel led Peter through the cells and out through the gates, which opened by themselves! Then the angel disappeared.

Peter hurried to the home where the believers were praying for him and knocked on the door. When a girl named Rhoda saw him at the door, she ran back and shouted, "Peter is here!"

They said, "Impossible! You must have seen his ghost."

Peter kept on knocking, and finally they came and let him in. He told them what had happened; then he went away to a safer place.

349
Travelling Disciples Start New Churches

Acts 13–15

Paul, who used to be called Saul, and Barnabas were two of the men chosen to preach the good news about Jesus to people in different countries. A young man, John Mark, went as their assistant.

They visited places in Greece and Turkey. In Turkey, John Mark decided to leave the other men and go home.

The preaching of Paul and Barnabas upset the Jews who didn't believe in Jesus. They got jealous because these new speakers were so popular. But the non-Jews were interested in the Good News, and many of them became Christians.

When a group of people trusted

350
The Church Solves a Problem

Acts 15–16

In the early part of the Bible, we read about how God taught his people to make animal sacrifices. These sacrifices were a kind of preview of the sacrifice of God's Son, Jesus, who would come many years later. Now that Jesus had come and had died as the sacrifice for the world's sin, did the Jews need to keep on making animal sacrifices? This was the question that the early Christians began to argue about. And did the Gentile Christians need to follow Jewish customs?

Finally the church leaders had a meeting. They prayed for wisdom and talked about these problems. God showed them that he did not expect them to make animal sacrifices. He said

Jesus, Paul and Barnabas organized them into a church and appointed a leader to help them understand more about Jesus.

Finally the two missionaries decided to go back and check up on all the new churches they had started. Barnabas wanted to take John Mark, but Paul said, "No. We can't depend on him."

They argued, and the argument separated Paul and Barnabas. Barnabas took John Mark and went to the island of Cyprus. Paul teamed up with Silas and went to Syria.

that Gentiles need not act like Jews but that Jewish and Gentile believers should be Christian brothers and sisters. The leaders sent letters explaining this to all the new churches. Paul and Silas went on travelling. They met new believers everywhere they went. Two of these became special friends of Paul's. Timothy, a young man in Lystra, became almost like a son to Paul. Lydia, a businesswoman in Philippi, shared her home with the apostles when they were in town.

— 351 —
Paul and Silas in Jail
Acts 16

Lydia often met with other Christians to pray beside a river in Philippi. Paul and Silas joined them. They often saw a slave girl who was in the power of evil spirits. Her owners got a lot of money by using her as a fortune-teller. She followed the apostles, shouting, "These men are servants of God. They will tell you how to have your sins forgiven."

One day Paul turned to her and said to the evil spirit, "In the name of Jesus Christ, come out of this girl!"

The spirit obeyed. The girl was free, but now she couldn't tell fortunes anymore. This made her owners angry. They dragged Paul and Silas before some judges. They didn't admit they were angry about losing money. They accused the apostles of teaching things that were against Roman law.

The judges ordered that the apostles be beaten and thrown into jail. They told the jailer, "We'll kill you if these prisoners escape!"

Paul and Silas spent the night praying and singing songs of praise.

352
A Helpful Earthquake

Acts 16

About midnight an earthquake shook the prison where Paul and Silas were being held. The doors flew open, and the prisoners' chains broke. When the jailer saw the prison standing wide open, he thought the prisoners had escaped. He knew he would be killed for letting them get away, so he picked up his sword to kill himself.

Paul called quickly, "Don't harm yourself. We are all here!" Even though they could have run away, all the prisoners had stayed in their cells!

The jailer fell down before Paul and Silas and said, "What can I do to be saved?"

They answered, "Just believe in the Lord Jesus Christ."

Then they told him the Good News about Jesus, and the jailer and his family believed. The judges then sent word that Paul and Silas could go free. But Paul said, "They beat us and imprisoned us without a trial. That was illegal because

we are Roman citizens. Let them come and release us themselves!"

The judges had not realized the apostles were Roman citizens. They were worried that they would get into trouble, so they came and apologized and begged the apostles to leave.

— 353 —
Paul's Preaching Starts Trouble

Acts 18–19

In Corinth, Paul made friends with a Christian couple, Aquila and Priscilla. They were tentmakers, just like Paul. Later Paul preached at Ephesus, doing miracles and leading many to believe in Jesus. Most of the people in Ephesus had worshipped the Greek goddess Diana. They bought silver idols of Diana to keep in their homes. When they became Christians they didn't worship the idols anymore.

Soon the men who made the idols were losing business. Demetrius, a silversmith, called a meeting and said, "We are losing much business because of Paul's preaching. We must get rid of him."

The silversmiths started a riot. Everyone shouted, "Great is Diana of the Ephesians!" An angry crowd tried to find Paul to attack him. But Paul's friends kept him safe.

The mayor of Ephesus got everyone's attention and said, "This isn't doing any good. If these preachers are breaking any laws, bring them before a court in the legal way. This riot will only get us into trouble with the Roman government. Calm down, and go home." The riot stopped, and the apostles were able to leave the city in safety.

354
More Christians and More Trouble
Acts 20–23

Once Paul was preaching on the third floor of a building. He talked until midnight. A young man sitting in an open window fell asleep and tumbled to the ground below. Everyone thought he was dead, but Paul picked him up, and he was all right! In Caesarea, Agabus, a prophet, warned Paul that if he returned to Jerusalem, he would be taken prisoner. Paul's friends tried to keep him from going, but Paul said he must go.

In Jerusalem Paul's enemies tried to kill him, but a Roman army captain protected him. Paul told the captain how he had become a Christian. Then Paul told him he was a Roman citizen. A Roman citizen was supposed to get a fair trial if he was suspected of a crime. Forty of Paul's enemies vowed not to eat or drink until they had killed Paul. They planned to kidnap him, but somehow Paul's nephew heard about their plot and warned Paul and the captain. The captain decided to send Paul to the Roman governor, Felix, in Caesarea. They went secretly, at night, to protect Paul from his enemies.

355
Paul Talks to Felix
Acts 23–24

The Roman captain sent a letter to Governor Felix, explaining about Paul's trouble. Felix read the letter and said to Paul, "When your accusers get here, I will listen to both sides of the story."

Several days later, the high priest arrived with some of the elders and a lawyer. They told Felix that Paul was a troublemaker who led a rebellion against the Roman government and defiled the Temple! Paul told Felix that the high priest had lied. Paul said, "I believe in the Jewish Law, and I respect the Temple. My conscience is clear."

Felix kept Paul in prison but was kind to him. Paul told Felix how he had become a Christian.

This made Felix nervous, and he sent Paul back to jail, but Felix talked with him often. Two years later a new governor named Festus came and took Felix's place.

356
Paul Appeals to Caesar

Acts 25–26

Paul's enemies tried to get the new governor, Festus, to send Paul back to Jerusalem to be tried. They thought they might have a chance to kill him before a trial could take place! But Festus refused. He said, "No, the man is in Caesarea. That is where we will try him."

Again Paul's enemies came and told lies about Paul, and again Paul denied them. Festus asked him, "Do you want to go to Jerusalem to continue this trial?"

"No!" Paul said. "I have a right to appear before Caesar, the Roman emperor."

"All right," Festus replied. "You shall have an audience with Caesar!"

King Agrippa visited Festus a few days later, and Festus told him all about Paul.

Paul told Agrippa about his turning to Jesus Christ and preached the gospel to him, but Agrippa was not convinced that the gospel was true. However, he could see that Paul was innocent of any crime.

Agrippa said to Festus, "If Paul hadn't insisted on appearing before Caesar, I would have released him. But now he will have to go to Rome."

The governor made arrangements for Paul to sail to Rome, carefully guarded by some soldiers.

357
A Storm and a Shipwreck
Acts 27

Festus put an officer named Julius in charge of Paul on the voyage to Rome. Strong winds drove the ship off course. The captain stopped at Myra and transferred his passengers to another ship headed for Rome.

The weather got worse, and the new ship's captain stopped at Fair Havens for several days. It was the wrong time of year to make such a voyage, and Paul advised the captain to stay in Fair Havens until spring.

The captain disagreed and sailed anyway. The storm got worse. The winds blew the ship far out to sea. For many days the crew fought to keep the ship from sinking. Finally, they lost all hope.

Paul said, "The Lord has promised me that no one will die, even though we will be shipwrecked."

Two weeks after the storm hit them, the ship was driven toward some rocks near land. The ship ran aground, and the rough waves began to tear it apart.

The soldiers thought Julius should kill the prisoners so they wouldn't escape, but he refused. Everyone jumped overboard, and just as God had promised, they all reached shore alive!

— 358 —
A Snake Bites Paul

Acts 28

When the sailors and their passengers got to the shore, they didn't know where they were. Many people who lived there came to help them. They said, "Welcome! This is the island of Malta."

They were very kind to the shipwrecked group. They started a fire on the beach to warm them and dry their clothes.

Paul helped gather wood for the fire. Suddenly a poisonous snake came out of the sticks, coiled itself around Paul's arm, and bit his hand.

"Aha!" cried the people. "This man must be a dangerous criminal. He was saved from the shipwreck, but he is going to be punished by death from this snakebite."

Paul held his arm out over the bonfire and shook the snake loose. Everyone expected Paul's arm to swell with the poison, but he showed no bad effects from the snakebite.

Then they said, "He's not a criminal. Maybe he's some kind of god!"

The governor of Malta, Publius, invited Paul and the other passengers to stay at his house. Paul healed Publius's father, who was sick with a fever. Many others who were sick were also healed by Paul.

— 359 —
Paul Lives in Rome

Acts 28

In the spring the ship's captain found another ship, and they continued their trip. They landed on the coast of Italy; then the soldiers and their prisoners

walked to Rome. Christians in Rome hurried out to welcome Paul. Once in Rome the guards turned their prisoners over to the Roman soldiers. For the next two years Paul lived in a house provided for him, but he wasn't allowed to leave the house, and guards watched him all the time.

Paul asked the local Jewish leaders to visit him. He said, "The Jews in Jerusalem wanted to kill me, but the Roman officials wanted to set me free because they could see I was innocent. To avoid a trial in Jerusalem, I demanded to be tried before Caesar, so they sent me here. I want to tell you about Jesus so you will understand what I believe."

Paul taught them about Jesus' love for them and his death and resurrection. A lot of them became Christians.

During the time he lived in Rome, Paul had many opportunities to preach and help people understand and accept the gospel.

360
Letters from the Apostles

Romans 6, 12–13;
1 Corinthians 1, 7, 12–14

Paul and the other apostles sent letters to encourage the believers in each church they had started and to tell them how to live. We call those letters the "Epistles". Paul wrote most of them.

When Paul wrote to the believers in Rome, he reminded them that all people are sinners but that if they would trust in Jesus Christ, God would take away their sins.

Paul told the Romans to serve God and love each other and their enemies. He taught them to obey the government and its laws.

When Paul wrote to the Corinthians, he said, "Don't quarrel and split up into unfriendly groups." He told them how

to have strong marriages, being pure and loving to one another. And he said each believer had his or her own special abilities to help the church and serve other people.

Paul said that if we love others, we will be patient and kind. We won't be jealous, envious, boastful, proud, selfish, or rude. We will always be loyal and defend those we love!

In every one of Paul's letters he promised that the Holy Spirit would give believers the power to live the right kind of lives.

361
The Christian Soldier's Armour

Ephesians 6

When Paul wrote to the Ephesian Christians, he reminded them that Satan is the worst enemy of God and God's people. Satan tries to stop us from doing right. It's like a long, hard war throughout our lives.

Paul advised the Ephesians to use the armour God gave them to defeat Satan.

Paul said that truth is like the wide belt that soldiers wore to protect the middle part of the body. And right living is like a breastplate that protects the heart. Faith is the shield that stops the arrows Satan shoots at us, and salvation is the helmet that protects our heads from injury. He said we can move away from Satan quickly if we wear the shoes of the good news of peace with God.

But the best weapon against Satan, Paul said, is the sword of the Spirit which is

the Word of God, the Bible.

And then he told them one more good way to win the battle with Satan: pray all the time!

362
Jesus is Coming Again

1 Thessalonians 4–5; 2 Thessalonians 2–3

Paul wrote two letters to the believers in Thessalonica, telling them about the promise that Jesus will return. He said that when Jesus is ready to return, he will appear in the sky and give a great shout of victory. An archangel will cry out loudly, and there will be a trumpet call.

The Christians who have already died will rise and be taken up into the sky to meet Jesus. After that, those on earth who love Jesus will rise into the sky too.

All believers will then be given new bodies, perfect and pure in every way, and they will be with Jesus forever.

Paul said that these amazing things will happen very quickly.

He wanted everyone to know about the future so we will not worry about what happens to Christians who die. They are safe in God's care.

Paul said believers must keep watching for Jesus and obeying God as they wait for that wonderful day. Those words are just as true today as they were then.

363

The Runaway Slave

Philemon

Once when Paul was in prison, he had a visitor named Onesimus. Paul told him about Jesus, and Onesimus became a Christian. He did many kind things for Paul, but he had a serious problem. Onesimus was a slave who had run away from his master. Paul was surprised to hear that the master was his friend Philemon. Long ago Paul had told Philemon about Jesus and Philemon had become a believer.

Onesimus decided he should return to Philemon and be his slave again. Paul was afraid that Philemon might punish Onesimus severely for running away.

Paul wrote a letter for Onesimus to take to Philemon. In the letter Paul thanked Philemon for helping the church and letting the believers meet in his home. He asked Philemon to be kind and forgiving to Onesimus.

Paul said, "Now that Onesimus is a believer too, you and he should be like brothers. If Onesimus owes you any money, I will repay it." Then he reminded Philemon how much he owed Paul for helping him find God. Nothing could repay that debt!

364
An Unsigned Letter

Hebrews

The writer of Hebrews wrote that Jesus Christ is like the high priests of the Old Testament. The high priest went into the Most Holy Place in the Temple and offered the blood from sacrificed animals. Then God forgave the sins of the people who had given those animals. When Jesus died to become our Saviour, he gave his own blood for our salvation, so God has forgiven us and we can go into his presence and speak to him in prayer.

The writer of Hebrews explained what real faith is. He said it is being sure something is going to happen even though we are not able to see it happening right now.

In Hebrews we read of people who had this kind of faith – Abel, Enoch, Noah, Abraham, Sarah, Jacob, Joseph, Moses and his parents, the Israelites who followed Moses out of Egypt, and the soldiers who marched around Jericho.

The writer said that we should live our lives as if we are running a race in a stadium and all those heroes of faith are watching and urging us on.

365

John's Vision of Heaven

Revelation

The apostle John was a prisoner on the island of Patmos. One morning he had a wonderful vision of Jesus in his glory. "His eyes were bright like flames of fire," John wrote. "His feet gleamed like polished bronze, and his voice was like thunder. His face shone like the sun."

Jesus said to John, "I am the Living One who died but is now alive."

He took John's spirit into heaven. John saw God sitting on a great throne. Light flashed from him. Lightning and thunder came from the throne. In front of it was a shining crystal sea. Then John heard millions of angels singing praise to God.

John saw terrible things happening on earth to people who refused to obey the Lord. But then he saw the Holy City.

He heard a voice shout, "God will live among the people, and they will belong to him. There will be no more death or sorrow."

An angel said, "Nothing impure will be allowed there. No one who does wrong can enter. Only those whose sins have been washed away by the death of the Lord Jesus Christ can come in. Their names are written in God's Book of Life."